Branson's Cookin'!

Celebrity Cookbook

From Branson's Best...Well, Most Famous Cooks!

4TH EDITION

Branson's Cookin'!

Celebrity Cookbook

Copyright© 1996
ISBN 0-9636666-9-X
$12.95
By Anderson Publishing, Inc.
Branson's Review Magazine
PO Box Box 357
Branson, Missouri 65615

This book includes the finest plastic ring binders available, but, like most plastics, the binders can be damaged by excessive heat, so avoid exposing them to the direct rays of the sun, or excessive heat such as in a car on a hot day, or on the top of the kitchen stove. If not exposed to heat, the binders will last indefinitely.

Welcome to Our Kitchen!

We started compiling these recipes over 9 years ago by publishing them in our magazine, "Branson's Country Review." Our idea was to use the recipes in a cookbook that we would print sometime in the future. Well, the future is now, and the cookbook is finally here.

I also understand why no one has ever done this before...it's a lot of work! Cookbooks are not an easy thing to do, and when you deal with entertainers and their schedules, to say nothing of their publicists and agents, well, some things do get pushed to the back burner.

You will also notice in these pages that the "stars" of this cookbook represent a wide variety of entertainers in Branson, some who are always in the limelight, and others who are sometimes in the limelight. It's not just the "star" entertainers who have made Branson what it is today, it is also the supporting cast who have won the hearts of fans. The friendliness that Branson's entertainers display cuts across the stage and the players you see on it. It's that friendliness that I wanted you to see here in this cookbook. It's not limited to that single person on the stage, and it's not limited to one act or one theatre. It is the group of us in Branson that makes the whole–there are not too many cooks here to spoil the broth. It just takes a variety of ingredients to make it this rich.

So, I hope you enjoy this 4th Edition of our cookbook, Branson is a wealth of talent on stage...and in the kitchen...well...most of these cooks will keep their night jobs-but you'll still love their recipes.

Enjoy Branson's Cookin'...

It'll taste like home!

Pass the vittles,

Edward Anderson, Publisher

Branson's Cookin'!
Celebrity Cookbook

I N D E X

ANDY WILLIAMS

One of the music world's greatest hit makers, Andy Williams performs two shows a day in his architectural masterpiece, the Moon River Theatre. Andy made a double hit when he came to Branson in 1992—his show was an immediate hit, and his involvement with the community was a hit with local residents.

In the course of his forty-plus-year, solo career, Andy has recorded more than 800 songs in seven languages—but naming his theatre after his signature song was irresistible. "Ever since I've been associated with *Moon River*, I thought it was a great name for a lot of things. It's a very romantic image."

"A" Is For Andy

Mama's Rhubarb Shortcake

Ingredients:

1-1/2 lbs. strawberry rhubarb
4 Tbsp. butter
1 C. milk
2 tsp. baking powder
2 loaf pans

1 C sugar (white)
1 egg (beaten)
2 C. flour
2 C. brown sugar

Instructions:

Cut rhubarb into 1-inch pieces.
Divide evenly into bottoms of loaf pans.
Pour one cup of brown sugar over each layer of rhubarb.

Make shortcake batter out of remaining ingredients:

Cream butter, sugar and beaten egg.
Add flour, milk and baking powder.

Pour batter (divided evenly) over rhubarb and brown sugar.

Bake one hour at 350 degrees.

Turn pans upside-down to cool. Serve in upside down position so that the rhubarb is on top.

Andy's Sweet & Hot Mustard

Ingredients:

1 Tbsp. Coleman's dry mustard
1 Tbsp. flour
3 Tbsp. sugar

Instructions:

Mix with boiling water and 1/2 tsp. of vinegar.

Use over cooked lamb or ham.

ANITA BRYANT

Hundreds of thousands of American servicemen first "met" Anita Bryant during her seven consecutive Christmas shows with Bob Hope overseas. On the home front, hits like *Paper Roses* and *Till There Was You* firmly established her as a vocal presence in the hearts of America.

All of her life, Anita Bryant has stood for God, country and family. Now appearing in a theatre of her very own—the "Anita Bryant Theatre" on 76 Country Boulevard—the entertainer, who has consistently been named as one of America's most-admired women, has found a home in Branson.

The combination was a natural!

Anita's Key Lime Pie
Serves 6

Crust:
1 cup graham cracker crumbs
2 tbsp. sugar
2 to 3 tbsp. melted butter or margarine

Filling:
1 can (15-oz.) condensed milk
3 egg yolks
1/2 cup lime juice

Topping:
1/2 pint heavy cream
2 tsp. powdered sugar
1 tsp. vanilla

Preheat oven to 350 degrees. In a bowl, combine ingredients for crust; firmly press into bottom and sides of a 9-inch pie plate. Bake 10 minutes; cool.

To make filling, in a bowl, combine all ingredients; blend well. Pour into cooled crust; refrigerate at least 1 hour.

To make topping, in a bowl, beat heavy cream until stiff peaks form; blend in sugar and vanilla. Spread over pie. Refrigerate before serving. Makes a 9-inch pie.

Anita's Baltimore Imperial Crab
Makes 4 servings

1 lb. crab meat
1 to 1-1/4 cups evaporated milk
2 eggs, well beaten
4 tbsp. or more of mayonnaise

Salt and pepper
Dry mustard to taste
Pimento

Combine all these ingredients and let stand about 2 hours. Preheat oven to 350 degrees. Pack in shells, let liquid drain off. Cover with mayonnaise, garnish with pimento. Bake 15 to 20 minutes; watch carefully!

BOBBY VINTON

Described as "the all-time most successful love singer of the 'rock era' " by *Billboard* Magazine, Bobby Vinton had more No. 1 hits between 1962 and 1972 than any other male vocalists, including *Roses Are Red*, *Mr. Lonely* and the hit Polish-Americans embraced as a new national anthem, *My Melody of Love*.

From the stage of his 1,300-seat, 76 Country Boulevard venue—the Blue Velvet Theatre—Bobby Vinton can still melt a heart...or make it beat faster. Joining him in the European-style theatre, complete with ceiling murals, Italian tile and blue velvet accents, is the incomparable sound of the Glenn Miller Orchestra.

Bobby Vinton – The "Polish Prince" Puts Some "Pnash" In His Cookin'!

GOTOMKI (gōWūmki)

Ingredients:

1 C. cooked rice
1 lb. mild pork sausage
1 med. onion
(chopped & saute til limp)

4 oz. can of mushrooms
1 tsp. paprika
1/2 C. milk, skim or low fat
1/4 C. water warm

3/4 lb. beef
1 egg
2 med. heads of cabbage (cut core so leaves will separate when boiled)
1 C (14-16 oz) tomato sauce
1/2 tsp. marjoram
2 Tbsp. flour
pepper & salt to taste

Instructions:
Place cabbage into large pot. Boil until leaves fall from head. Set leaves aside. Saute chopped onions with mushrooms. Add onions and mushrooms to cooked rice, beef, and pork. Mix. Add egg, paprika, marjoram, milk, water, flour, pepper and salt. Fold mixture so ingredients are thoroughly mixed. Spoon and place mixture into the center of one cabbage leaf. Fold one side of the leaf over mixture and remaining side over the folded leaf to enclose mixture and create a cabbage roll. Repeat. Place gotomki in a large tray in single rolls (To keep gotomki from opening place "seam" down.) Cover with aluminum foil. Bake at 350°F for 2 hours or until gotomki can be cut with a fork. When gotomki can be cut with a fork, pour tomato sauce over rolls. Re-cover with aluminum foil and bake at 300°F for 3/4 hour. Yields about 2 dozen, depending on the size of the cabbage leaves.

Bobby' Blue Velvet Dessert

Ingredients:
PIEROGO
1-1/2 C. flour
1 Tbsp. warm water
sour cream, sugar or plain yogurt

1/2 C. mashed potatoes
1 pt. blueberries

Instructions:
Boil potatoes until soft. Mash. Add to flour. Mix with fork. Add water. (If 1 tbsp. is not sufficient to make a pasta-like dough add a tad more until consistency is smooth enough to roll out dough.) Roll dough mixture till thickness is about 1/8" to 1/4" thick. Cut dough into 3-inch circles (using the rim of a regular glass will do this job well). Spoon blueberries onto dough. Fold dough over blueberries, pinching ends with your thumb and index finger or use a fork to seal the berries in. If ends of dough do not adhere, water fingertips and squeeze dough again. Repeat. Drop Pierogies into boiling water. When pierogies rise to the top, cook for 3 additional minutes or until desired tenderness is achieved. Top with sour cream, sugar, or plain yogurt. Blueberries may be substituted with sliced apples, apricots, strawberries.

The BV Special

(Grilled Polish Sausage Appetizer)

Ingredients:
Brown Bread
Polish Sausage

Apple Butter
Mild Cheese

Instructions:
Take small slices of brown bread and spread with apple butter.
Grill sausage. Top bread with 1/4" slice of Polish sausage.
Follow with topping of small slice of mild cheese. Bake in the oven for 10 minutes at 350°.

BARBARA FAIRCHILD

Barbara Fairchild is no stranger to the world of music and entertainment. A two-time Grammy nominee, she established herself in the early 70s as a major artist in the country music field; she is now having a powerful impact on the gospel music of the 90s.

A long-time Branson favorite—both in her shows or at her Sunday morning Worship Services—the star acquired her own '76 Country Boulevard' Theatre in 1996, after years of appearing at the theatres of local celebrities like Mel Tillis and Jim Stafford.

Barbara says about her Ozark home, "I love this town, and I love what this town stands for. Branson offers more than rare entertainment—more than a wholesome destination for families. Branson is a place touched by God."

LASAGNA

2 lb. Italian sausage
1 large can tomatoes
2 small cans tomato paste
4 to 6 cloves garlic, minced
1 tbsp. parsley, chopped
1 tbsp. basil, chopped
1-1/2 to 2 tsp. salt
1 tbsp. olive oil
2 8-oz. ctn. small curd
   cottage or Ricotta cheese

2 beaten eggs
1 cup Parmesan cheese
2 tbsp. parsley, chopped
1/2 tsp. black pepper
2 tsp. salt
2 pkg. slice Mozzarella
Wide lasagna noodles
   (6 to 7)

Cook sausage; pour off grease. Add tomatoes, tomato paste, garlic, 1 tablespoon chopped parsley, basil, 1-1/2 to 2 tsp. salt and olive oil. Simmer until thickened.

Mix cottage cheese, eggs, Parmesan cheese, 2 tbsp. chopped parsley, pepper and last 2 tsp. of salt.

In large pan, make layers of noodles, 1/2 cheese mixture, 1 pkg. Mozzarella and 1/2 meat mixture. Repeat layers. Bake at 375-degrees for 30 minutes. Let stand at least 15 minutes. Even better the next day.

DELMONICO POTATOES

9 medium potatoes
Salt
1/3 cup butter or margarine
2-1/4 c. light cream or milk
   (2% milk for low-fat side dish)
1 4-oz. pkg. shredded Cheddar or other cheese (1 cup)

1/8 tsp. pepper
3 tbsp. dried bread crumbs
1/3 cup flour

Cook potatoes with 1 tsp. salt until fork tender. Drain and cool. About 1 hour before serving, preheat oven to 375. Peel and dice potatoes.

In large saucepan, over medium heat, melt butter. With wire whisk or slotted spoon, stir in flour until smooth. Gradually add cream or milk and cook, stirring constantly, until mixture is thick and bubbling. Stir in 2 tsp. salt and 1/8 tsp. pepper. Gently stir in potatoes. Pour mixture into greased 12x8-inch baking dish; sprinkle with cheese, then bread crumbs. Bake 25 minutes until cheese is melted and mixture is bubbly.

FRIED TOMATOES
(Serves 4)

4 medium size tomatoes
1 egg, beaten
1 cup flour
Salt to taste
Bread crumbs
Brown sugar

Slice tomatoes 1/2-inch thick. Dip slices in flour; then dip into egg batter; and then in bread crumbs. Fry in greased pan, browning on both sides. Sprinkle brown sugar on each side as you place them on platter after frying.

ANGEL BISCUITS

5 cups flour
3/4 cup shortening
   (butter flavor)
1 tsp. soda
1 tsp. salt
3 tsp. baking powder
3 tbsp. sugar
1 yeast cake, dissolved
   in 1/2 cup warm water
2 cups buttermilk

Sift dry ingredients together. Cut in shortening until mixed thoroughly. Add buttermilk and dissolved yeast. Work together with large spoon until all flour is moistened. Cover bowl and place in refrigerator until ready to use (best after it sets overnight).
When ready to use, take out as much as needed. Work on floured board as you would any other biscuit. Bake at 400 for about 12 minutes, or until golden brown.

BoxCar Willie

All aboard! America's favorite hobo conducts audiences on a nostalgic tour of hard-core country music. The first celebrity entertainer to buy a theatre and perform on a permanent basis in Branson (in 1987), BoxCar Willie is a 22-year Veteran of the U.S.A.F. In his shows, a salute to fellow Veterans joins a repertoire of railroad songs, Hank Williams Sr. songs and a lively collection of his own material.

A reporter once asked BoxCar why people come to Branson. He gave the reporter a long look and said, "Why would anyone NOT come to Branson? That's a better question!"

You Won't Find This Food In The Hobo Jungle!

BoxCar's Cranberry Salad

Ingredients:

1 pkg. cranberries
1-1/2 C. sugar
1 pkg. marshmallows
1/2 C. chopped nuts

1 Tbsp. of gelatin
1/2 C. cold water
1-1/2 C. whipped cream

Instructions:

Grind cranberries, add sugar, marshmallows, and nuts to cranberries. Mix gelatin and cold water in saucepan. Dissolve over medium heat. Add gelatin to cranberry mixture, set in refrigerator until mixture begins to jell. Fold in whipped cream. Mold and chill.

BoxCar's Peach Delight

Ingredients:

1 box peach Jello
3/4 C. boiling water
2 C. of ice cubes

Cool Whip
1 can of peaches
   (crushed or chopped)

Instructions:

Mix all ingredients together and put in graham cracker crust. Freeze until set, then keep in refrigerator.

BoxCar's Sour Cream Corn Bread

Ingredients:

1 C self rising corn meal
2 eggs
18-3/4 oz. cream corn

1 C. sour cream
1/2 C. salad oil

Instructions:

Combine all ingredients, mixing well. Pour into greased 9" pan. Bake at 400 degrees for 20 - 30 minutes.

BoxCar's Broccoli Casserole

Ingredients:

1 (10 oz.) pkg. broccoli
1/2 can of evaporated
  milk or reg. milk
1/2 lb. of Velveeta cheese
  (diced or grated)

1 can of cream of
  mushroom soup
1 medium onion (chopped)
1 stick butter (1/2 C)
1-1/2 cup cooked rice

Instructions:

Saute onion while butter is melting. Mix together. Bake 1 hour at 350 degrees.

BoxCar's Homemade Vanilla Ice Cream

Ingredients:

4 eggs
2-1/2 cups of sugar
6 cups of milk

4 cups of cream
3 Tbsp. of vanilla
1/2 tsp. of salt

Instructions:

Beat eggs until light. Add sugar gradually. When mixture thickens, add milk, cream, vanilla, and salt. Mix thoroughly and pour into freezer.

Chill mixture for several hours or overnight. Hope You Enjoy!

BoxCar's Peanut Butter Balls

Ingredients:

1 stick margarine (soften)
2 cups chunky peanut butter

1 lb. box powdered sugar
3 cups Rice Krispies

Instructions:

Mix together and form into small balls. Melt large Hershey bar and 6 oz. package of chocolate chips with small slab of paraffin. Dip balls in chocolate mixture and place on wax paper until cool.

BUCK TRENT

"Oh Yeah!"

When Buck Trent says those two magic words and gives his famous "thumbs up" signal, you know you can sit back and get set for a world-class performance of spectacular banjo pickin' and relaxed country humor— as well as a look at some of the most dazzling jackets in town!

Twice-named CMA " Instrumentalist of the Year," Buck has also twice been named the No. 1 "Instrumentalist of the Year" for the Music City Awards.

He's no newcomer to town, either. "I was in Branson the first time in 1973, playing with Porter (Wagoner). He and Dolly (Parton) worked at the Baldknobbers. Now, it's great to be in Branson because everybody that comes here wants to live here. They're like my kinfolk!"

Buck Trent – You, Too, Can Say "Oh, Yeah!" To His Cooking!

Buck's No Bake Peanut Butter Cookies

In saucepan combine 2 cups sugar and 2/3 cups milk and boil 3 minutes. Remove from heat. Add 6 heaping Tbsp. crunchy peanut butter, 1 tsp. vanilla.

Mix well, add 1/4 lb. soda crackers (crushed-not too fine). Stir until completely mixed and heated through. Drop by spoonful on waxed paper (work fast!) Let set and cool. Most pound boxes of crackers have 4 packages. Use one package.

Buck's Okra-Tomato Casserole

Ingredients:

6 C. sliced tender okra
1/2 C. chopped onion
1/2 tsp. salt
1 Tbsp. dry butter substitute

3 med. fresh tomatoes, chopped
1/2 C. chopped green pepper
1/4 tsp. pepper

Place layers of okra, tomatoes, onion, green pepper in non-stick 2-quart casserole. Repeat layers. Top with dry butter substitute. Bake at 350 degrees for one hour.

Buck's Sweet Potato Casserole

Instructions:

2 C. grated raw sweet potato
1 C. sugar
1 C. milk

1 Tbsp. flour
2 eggs
1/2 C. butter

Mix eggs, sugar, flour, and milk. Beat until smooth. Add grated potatoes. Pour into buttered baking dish. Dot top with butter. Bake at 375 degrees for 45 minutes. Serves 6 - 8.

Buck's Barbeque Sauce

Ingredients:

1 qt. catsup (Del Monte or Heinz)
1 tsp. barbeque seasoning spice
2 Tbsp. chili powder
2 Tbsp. Wrights Liquid Smoke

1 Tbsp. salt
1 Tbsp. pepper
1/2 qt. vinegar (apple cider)

Instructions:

Tabasco to taste. Mix all in sauce pan and cook over medium to low heat until mixture thickens.

Buck's Marshmallow Fudge Cake

Ingredients:

2 C. flour
2 C. sugar
1 stick butter
1 C. water
1/2 C. Wesson Oil
4 Tbsp. cocoa

1 tsp. baking soda
1 tsp. vanilla
2 Tbsp. cinnamon
2 eggs beaten
1/2 C. buttermilk

Instructions:

In large mixing bowl add flour and sugar.

Mix and heat in saucepan the following:
1 stick butter, 1 cup of water, 1/2 cup Wesson oil, and 4 Tbsp. cocoa.

Pour heated mixture into flour mixture. Add 2 beaten eggs. Add 1/2 cup buttermilk with 1 tsp. baking soda whipped in. Add 1 tsp. vanilla and 2 Tbsp. cinnamon.

Grease a 9"x13" glass oblong pan. Pour mixture into glass pan. Bake at 300 degrees for 30 minutes.

Five minutes before cake is done, start fudge icing.

1 stick butter
2 Tbsp. milk
4 Tbsp. cocoa

2 C. powdered sugar (one box)
1 tsp. vanilla
1 C. chopped pecans

Mix and bring to a boil in saucepan.

Pour over 2 cups powdered sugar (one box) and beat until smooth. Put two cups miniature marshmallows on top of cake. Add 1 tsp. vanilla and 1 cup chopped pecans. Pour icing mixture over marshmallows and blend together. Makes 12 large pieces.

CLIFF BRASCHLER

C liff Braschler is referred to as "The Old Man" of the Braschler Music Show. He is co-owner and sings first tenor on the musical variety show, which now airs from a new, state-of-the-art theater on Shepherd of the Hills Expressway.

His road to Branson began in St. James, Mo., and his path to the hill-top, jewel-box theatre wound through a Branson roll-call of musical history—the Lowe Theater and Music Land, U.S.A.

A minister in the Church of God, Cliff is still active in work and can be heard on most Sunday mornings conducting services at a variety of locations.

The Braschlers have been entertaining in Branson for over 12 years now
Cliff - The "Old" Man is pictured at the upper right.

Cliff's Brownies

Ingredients:
1 C. margarine softened
1 C. granulated sugar
4 eggs, lightly beaten
1 tsp. vanilla
1 C. plus 1 Tbsp. flour
1 (12 oz.) can chocolate syrup
1/2 C. chopped walnuts

Instructions:
Combine margarine and sugar and beat until fluffy. Add eggs and vanilla. Mix well. Stir in flour. Add chocolate syrup and chopped nuts. Mix until just blended. Bake in lightly greased 11 x 13-inch pan at 350 degrees for 25 - 30 minutes. Cool thoroughly. Slice and serve.

Cliff's Microwave Trout

Place six fresh rainbow trout filets on microwave tray. Dot with butter or margarine, or brush lightly with melted butter. Salt to taste. Sprinkle lightly with lemon-pepper seasoning. Microwave on high temperature 7 - 10 minutes or until fish becomes lightly crusted around the edges. Delicious!

Cliff's Chocolate Chip Oatmeal Cookies

Ingredients:
1 C. shortening
3/4 C. brown sugar, firmly packed
3/4 C. granulated sugar
1 tsp. salt
1 tsp. vanilla
2 eggs, lightly beaten
1 tsp. hot water
1-1/2 C. flour
2 C. oatmeal
1 tsp. baking soda
1 C. walnuts, coarsely chopped
1 (12 oz.) pkg. chocolate chips

Instructions:
Cream shortening and sugars together until fluffy. Add eggs, vanilla and hot water. Mix well. Combine flour, baking soda and salt. Add to sugar mixture. Add oatmeal, nuts and chocolate chips, mixing well. Drop by well rounded teaspoonful onto lightly greased baking sheet. Bake in 350 degree oven 8 - 10 minutes until lightly brown. Cool on wire rack. Yield approx. 4 dozen.

DINO KARTSONAKIS

Known as musicdom's premier piano virtuoso, Dino (*Chariots of Fire*) Kartsonakis says he never even considered doing anything else. From the first time he played a wobbly C-chord on a piano, he says his whole life's labor was set in motion.

"Did you ever experience something that was so vivid, so bold and impacting that you wanted to grab hold of it and never let go?," he says of his introduction to the piano at age three. "It was like God's hand touching me and launching my whole life."

Performing now at Branson's "Grand Palace"—including his all-stops-pulled "Christmas Extravaganza"—his return to the stage in Branson is always looked forward to and often sold out.

DINO'S TOMATO SALAD
Greek: Domata Salada

8 to 10 tomatoes
1 cucumber
1 tsp. oregano
1/2 lb. Feta, crumbled
5 green onions, chopped
2 cloves garlic, minced
1/4 cup olive oil

Cut tomatoes into wedges. Peel cucumbers and slice. Place in bowl. Add green onions, garlic, oregano and olive oil. Toss. Add Feta. Toss again. Serve with bread.

Dressing for Tomato Salad: 1/2 cup olive oil; 1/4 tsp. salt; juice of 1 lemon; and 1/4 tsp. oregano. Mix together and toss into the salad.

SPINACH CHEESE ROLLS
Greek: Spanakopetes

1 medium onion, finely chopped
1/2 cup olive oil
1 pkg. frozen chopped spinach,
    thawed; or 1 lb. fresh, well
    washed and finely chopped
1/2 lb. Feta cheese
6 oz. pot cheese
3 eggs, beaten
1/4 cup bread crumbs
1/2 lb. phyllo pastry sheets
1/2 cup butter, melted
    (half margarine may be used)

Spinach Cheese Rolls continued

Saute onion in olive oil for minutes. Add spinach, from which as much water as possible has been drained. Simmer with the onion over a low flame, stirring occasionally, until most of moisture is evaporated.

Crumble Feta cheese into small pieces. Add pot cheese and blend well. Add beaten eggs and mix well. Toss bread crumbs into spinach-onion mixture and add to cheese, stir until well blended.

Cut the sheets of phyllo pastry into quarters. Refrigerate 3 quarters and cover the 1 quarter with a lightly damped towel. Brush each quarter sheet well with melted butter.

Place 1 tablespoon of the spinach cheese 1 inch from narrow edge of sheet. Fold the inch margin over mixture; fold long edges in toward middle. Butter again and roll compactly to end. Bake the spanakopetes in a 425-degree oven for 20 minutes or until golden brown. Allow to cool about 5 minutes before serving. Serve warm. Yield: 40 to 50 pieces.
Note: This recipe may be made with American pie dough in a pie pan. Serve in pie wedges.

Rice Pudding
Greek: Rizogalo (Serves 8)

1/2 cup rice
1/2 quart water
1 quart milk
4 egg yolks
1 cup sugar
1 tsp. salt
Cinnamon to taste

Simmer rice in water and milk for about 45 minutes, or until sauce is thick and rice is soft. Beat egg yolks and sugar until thick and pale in color. Gradually stir in rice pudding; mix well and return to saucepan. Add salt and cook over low heat for about 2 minutes, stirring constantly to prevent curdling. Pour into pudding dishes and sprinkle with cinnamon. (1/2 cup raisins or a little grated lemon rind may be added.)

DOLLY PARTON

In the summer of 1995, Dolly Parton came to town to throw open the doors of her new dinner attraction, the Dixie Stampede. This unique dinner show—an alluring mix of rowdy family picnic and wild-west show—features a bountiful country dinner and a friendly rivalry that re-matches the South and the North in equestrian competition.

"Because of my career, I will not be able to personally be in Branson every day," said Dolly, "but through the Dixie Stampede I can achieve my goal of providing outstanding entertainment of which Branson can be proud."

DOLLY'S "ISLANDS IN THE STREAM"

Ingredients
3 eggs, separated
2/3 cup sugar
2 tsp. flour, heaping
1 quart milk
1 tsp. vanilla
nutmeg (optional)

Instructions
Cream egg yolks with sugar and whip until smooth. Add flour and mix well. Scald the milk, and when hot enough, add the creamed mixture. Stirring constantly, cook 20 to 25 minutes, until it thickens. Remove from heat and add vanilla.

Boil some water. Whip egg whites and add to water until hardened. Remove with spatula and put on top of the cream mixture. Sprinkle with nutmeg and chill.

DOUG GABRIEL

O ne of Branson's most popular morning show artists, Doug Gabriel is a gentle man with a giant of a voice who's been delivering a wonder-filled wake up call to Branson audiences for several years. A 1996 move to the Roy Clark Celebrity Theatre has not only given Doug the morning headliner slot, but also a shot at over 80 evening dates during the year.

Branson star Roy Clark is pleased to have Doug performing at his theatre, and has said "Doug has really proved himself as a top Branson talent. When you hear this man sing, you'll know the sky is the limit!"

Backed in his show by his talented wife, Cheryl, Doug hits the stage and delivers 100% entertainment—and 150% of himself!

DOUG'S MEAT & POTATO PIE

Ingredients

1 lb. ground beef
1 egg
1/8 tsp. pepper
1/4 C. catsup
1/2 C. shedded sharp cheddar cheese

Potatoe buds (8 serving)
1 tsp. salt
1 Tbsp. onion
1 C. milk

Instructions

Heat oven at 350°. Lightly mix gorund beef, 1-1/3 cup potatoe buds, egg, salt, pepper, onion, catsup and milk. Spread evenly in 9" pie pan. Bake 35 - 40 minutes. Prepare remaining potatoe buds as directed on package for (4 servings) Pile mashed potatoes on baked meat loaf as a merinque on a pie. Sprinkle cheese over potatoes. Bake 3-4 minutes longer or until cheese melts. Serves 4 - 5.

GARY PRESLEY

That unforgettable Presley's Jubilee character, 'Herkimer,' was born when his portrayer was quite young. Gary Presley began his musical career when he was four years old and his parents stood him in a chair so he could reach the microphone to sing "Rudolph the Red-Nosed Reindeer."

Since every traditional country music group had a comedian, Gary created 'Herkimer'— he of the gap-toothed smile and subtly-pointed wit. After playing a series of shows in a cave and at many community gatherings, his father, Lloyd Presley decided that west 76 highway— outside of Branson—would be a good place to build a theatre. And oh boy, was he right! The rest is history—the history of 76 Country Boulevard and the "country music capital of the universe."

Gary Presley – "Herkimer's Handy Hints" For Home Cooking

PEANUT BUTTER KISSES

Ingredients

1 C granulated sugar
1 C packed brown sugar
1 C shortening
1 C Jif Peanut Butter
2 eggs
pieces
1/4 C milk

2 tsp. vanilla
3-1/2 C sifted flour
2 tsp. baking soda
1 tsp. salt
1 (11 oz.) pkg. milk chocolate

Instructions

Preheat oven to 375°. Cream together sugars, shortening and peanut butter. Add eggs, milk and vanilla; beat well. Stir together flour, baking soda and salt; add to Jif mixture. Beat well

Shape into 1-inch balls; roll in granulated sugar. Place on ungreased cookie sheet. Bake in 375° oven for 8 minutes. Remove from oven. Press a milk chocolate candy into center of each warm cookie. Return to oven; bake 3 minutes.

HONEY CHICKEN

Ingredients

1/2 C butter, melted
1/2 C honey
1/4 C prepared mustard

2 Tbsp. lemon juice
1 (2 - 3 lb.) fryer cut up
salt and pepper

Instructions

Combine butter, honey, mustard and lemon juice; stir well. Lightly sprinkle chicken with salt and pepper; place chicken, meaty side down, in a lightly greased 13 x 9 x 2 inch baking pan. Pour honey mixture over chicken; cover and refrigerate 3 to 4 hours.

Remove from refrigerator; bake covered at 350 ° for 30 minutes. Remove cover and turn chicken pieces; bake 30 minutes longer or until done, basting occasionally with pan drippings.

SESAME CHICKEN

Ingredients

1 egg beaten
1/4 C milk
1/2 C fine, dry bread crumbs
1/4 C sesame seeds
3/4 tsp. salt

1/4 tsp. pepper
3 whole chicken breasts,
    split, skinned and boned
1/2 C. all purpose flour
vegetable oil

Combine egg and milk; stir well. Combine breadcrumbs, sesame seeds, salt and pepper, stirring well. Dredge chicken in flour; dip in egg mixture, and dredge in bread crumbs mixture. Heat 1 inch of oil in a large skillet to 325°; add chicken, and fry 5 minutes on each side.

CREAMY POTATO BAKE

Ingredients

3 C. mashed potatoes
5 - 6 slices bacon, cooked
    and crumbled

1 (8 oz.) carton sour cream
3 sm. green onions, chopped
1 C. (4 oz.) shredded cheddar cheese

Instructions

Spread potatoes evenly in a lightly greased 10"x6"x2" baking dish; top with sour cream; sprinkle with bacon and green onion. Top with cheese. Bake at 300° for 30 minutes.

PECAN BARS

Ingredients

1-1/3 C. all purpose flour
2 Tbsp. brown sugar
1/2 C. butter or margarine, softened
1/2 C. firmly packed brown sugar
2 eggs

1/2 C. dark corn syrup
2 Tbsp. butter or margarine, melted
1/8 tsp. salt
3/4 C .chopped pecans

Instructions

Combine flour and 2 Tbsp. brown sugar. Cut in 1/2 cup butter with pastry blender until mixture resembles course meal. Press mixture evenly into a greased 9-inch square pan. Bake at 350° for 15 or 17 minutes.

Combine next ingredients, beating well. Stir in pecans. Pour fillings over prepared crust. Bake at 350° for 25 minutes.

GLEN CAMPBELL

After more than 25 years as one of the most successful stars in the music business, Glen says it's not the stardom that drives him. "I'm a musician—a guitar player and a singer," he explains. "And I love playing—that's the fun of it!"

In 1992, Glen signed with the Grand Palace to headline what was then Branson's newest theatre. Two years later he opened at a new, state-of-the-art theatre built to his specifications—The Glen Campbell Goodtime Theatre.

From Wichita to Phoenix, Galveston to Branson...The star can throw together a hearty meal that would satisfy anyone—from a Wichita lineman to a rhinestone cowboy!

Glen is pictured here with another Arkansas native musician, Violet Hensley, a well-known fiddle maker featured at Silver Dollar City.

Glen's Favorite Chili
(Makes 4 quarts)

Ingredients

1/2 lb. dry pinto beans
5 cups tomatoes,
   canned and peeled
1 lb. green peppers,
   seeded and chopped
1-1/2 lb. onions
   peeled and chopped
2 cloves garlic, crushed
1-1/2 tbsp. olive oil
1/2 cup parsley, minced
2-1/2 lb. ground beef
1 lb. ground pork
1/3 cup chili powder
2 tbsp. salt
1-1/2 tsp. pepper
1-1/2 tsp. cumin seed

Instructions

Soak pinto beans overnight in cold water (use large chili pot).

Cover beans with fresh cold water and simmer for two hours.
Saute green bell peppers, onions, garlic, and parsley in olive
oil, then brown pork and beef and add spices; cook for 10
minutes. Combine all the above with beans and cook
uncovered for one hour. Uncover and cook for another 30
minutes (add water if needed).

Glen's Chicken Casserole

Ingredients
1 tbsp. butter
1 onion, chopped
1 green pepper,
   chopped
1 4-oz. jar pimentos,
   including juice
2 cans cream of chicken soup
4 chicken breasts, boiled
   and cut into bite-size pieces
1 7-oz. ready-cut spaghetti
1 package grated cheese

Instructions
   Saute onion and peppers in butter. In a large mixing bowl add
your cream of chicken soup, pimentos, onions, peppers and bite-
sized cooked chicken. Mix your cooked 7 oz. ready cut spaghetti.
Mix all the ingredients together and pour into a 9"x13" baking dish
and top with grated cheese. Bake at 350 for 30 minutes.

DARRELL AND ROSIE PLUMMER

A vital part of the Branson music scene for 17 years, Darrell and Rosie Plummer have made music together for decades. The two met when Darrell was barely 16 and Rosie was 14, when he was playing his first "for pay" guitar gig with the Smokey Mountain Playboys in Winegarden, Missouri. The two married several years later.

Acquiring a theater on 76 Country Boulevard in Branson, the Plummer family—including son Randy and daughter Melody—entertained hundreds of thousands of country music fans. In 1990 they decided it was time to slow down and sold their venue to Moe Bandy.

After several quiet years, the Plummers realized that not entertaining left too big a hole in their lives and have embarked on a new road show, with the occasional—and popular—stop in Branson.

Cooking Up A Cold Weather Feast
With Rosie Plummer

CHICKEN AND FAVORITE DUMPLINGS

3 1/2 lb. stewing chicken   3 chopped celery stalks
1 med. onion, chopped

Disjoint chicken or leave whole. Place in deep Dutch oven and cover with water. Add celery and onions, and salt and pepper to taste. Simmer slowly two hours until chicken falls from the bone easily when pried with a fork. Debone chicken, reserving broth. Bring broth to a boil and drop dumplings in one at a time. Simmer until done, about 20 minutes.

FAVORITE DUMPLINGS

1 C. flour
1/4 tsp. baking powder
salt to taste
1/4 C. shortening or margarine
1 egg

Sift dry ingredients together once. Blend in shortening and egg. Mix well and roll out very thin.

HAMBURGER VEGETABLE SOUP

1 lb. ground beef   1 C. chopped onion
1 C. diced potatoes   1 C. sliced carrots
1 C. diced celery   4 C. tomatoes
3 C. water   1/4 C. uncooked rice
1/4 tsp. basil   1/4 tsp. thyme
Salt to taste

Cook the ground beef and onion together until all of the pink color has disappeared and the meat is lightly browned. Drain off excess fat. Add all other ingredients and bring to a boil. Simmer for 1 hour.

Holiday Cherry Salad

1 (3 oz) pkg. cherry gelatin   1 can cherry pie filling

Dissolve gelatin in one cup boiling water. Add cherry pie filling and stir to blend. Place in pretty serving dish and chill. This salad is easy to make and keeps well in the refrigerator.

Traditional Party Mix

1/4 C. butter or margarine   1-1/4 tsp. seasoned salt
4-1/2 tsp. Worcestershire sauce   2-2/3 C. Corn Chex cereal
2-2/3 C. Wheat Chex cereal   2-2/3 C. Rice Chex cereal
1 C. salted mixed nuts   1 C. pretzel sticks

Preheat oven to 250 degrees. In open roasting pan melt margarine in oven. Remove. Stir in seasoned salt and Worcestershire. Gradually add cereals, nuts and pretzels, stirring until all pieces are evenly coated. Bake 1 hour, stirring every 15 minutes. Spread on absorbent paper to cool. Store in airtight container.

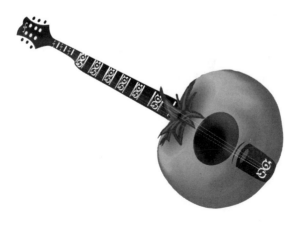

BESSIE MAE PRESLEY

Bessie Mae Presley—wife of Ozarks country music legend and father of the Presley clan, Lloyd Presley—has been involved in country music "forever." Considering that the Presleys were the first to build a theatre out 'in the boonies' of West Hwy. 76, she has also witnessed first-hand the phenomenal growth of both Branson and her family's business.

For over half a century Bessie Mae has fed the Presleys delicious-but-simple dishes from Lloyd's daily fish catch. The family gathers in her home often. She doesn't claim that her cooking is what brings the family together—but she admits it's an extra bonus.

BESSIE'S FAVORITE FISH RECIPE

Salt fish and roll in white corn meal. Fry in "real hot fat". That may sound easy, but just try it. This recipe proves that sometimes the simpler things in life are best. Bessie says this is her favorite.

ANOTHER RECIPE FOR COOKING FISH

Beat one egg, add a tiny bit of milk, mix 1/4 cup flour with 3/4 cup corn meal. Dip fish in egg batter, then roll in flour and corn meal mixture and deep fry.

FOGGY RIVER BOYS

The Foggy River Boys, named for the mist-covered Cumberland River of Nashville fame, go all the way back to a day when they were called the "Jordanaires." In those days, gospel singers didn't dare sing country songs in public, so the popular group recorded under the name of "Foggy River Boys."

A Branson favorite for many years, the group decided to retire in 1992 and sold their theatre. They still make special appearances in and around the Branson area—much to the continuing delight of their thousands of fans.

AUTOGRAPHS

Foggy River Boys - Great Harmony In The Kitchen, Too!

Jerry Dykes

14 oz. can dried black-eyed peas diced: bell pepper, 2 jalapeno peppers, 1/4 C. red onions, small jar pimentos. Season to taste with garlic, black pepper and salt. Chill and serve.

Cherry Cheese Cake

Don Shelton

2 lbs. cottage cheese	2 tbsp. flour
6 eggs	1 tbsp. cornstarch
1-3/4 c. confectioners sugar	1/2 pint heavy cream
2 tbsp. Lemon juice	1/2 pint milk
1 tsp. vanilla	l read crumbs

Add 1 egg at a time to cheese. Beat well. Add sugar, flour, cornstarch and flavoring. Beat in electric mixer 3 to 5 minutes, until light. Add cream and milk and beat for 5 minutes more. Pour into buttered spring pan, lined with bread crumbs on sides and bottom. Bake 1 hour in 350° oven. Cool in oven.

Cherry Glaze

1 can Bing cherries   2 tbsp. cornstarch   sugar to taste

Drain cherries and remove pits. Bring juice, sugar and cornstarch to boil. When thick, remove from stove, add cherries and cool. When cake is cold, remove from pan and cover top with cool, thickened cherry glaze. Chill and keep refrigerated.

Depression Fruit Cake

Denzel's Favorite Recipe

1 cup raisins stewed in 2 cups water until lone cup liquid remains.

Cream 1 cup sugar, 2 tbsp. shortening. Now add raisins and liquid. Sift 2 cups flour, 2 tsp. cinnamon, 1 tsp. nutmeg, 1 level tsp. soda, pinch salt, 1 cup walnuts. Mix all ingredients. Bake in loaf pan 350° until tests done.

FRIED SARDINES

Denzel Koontz

Denzel's mother used to cook canned sardines in tomato sauce, roll in flour, brown in .skillet. Serve as main meat dish with biscuits and gravy.

4-LAYER DESSERT

Mike Patrick

1st LAYER
1 stick melted butter
1 c. flour
1/2 c. pecans chopped
Pinch of salt
Mix together, press in
9 x 13 pan and bake
15 minutes at 350°.

2nd LAYER
8 oz. cream cheese
1 c. powdered sugar
1 c. Cool Whip
Mix together, spread on layer 1
and refrigerate for 15 minutes

3rd Layer
2 small boxes instant chocolate pudding   3 c. milk
(can use lemon, vanilla or butterscotch)   1 tsp. vanilla
Mix together, spread over layer 2 and refrigerate 15 minutes.

4th LAYER
Cover pudding with Cool Whip and sprinkle with pecans. Keep refrigerated.

JANIE FRICKE

Awards. Appearances. Twenty-three albums and 36 hit singles. Three years as a regular on the Nashville Networks' popular series, "The Statler Brothers Show." Singing in the White House before three Presidents; Ford, Reagan and Bush.

And Janie Fricke's still singing. But now, her stirring voice, heartfelt style and lively performances are endearing her to the audiences of Branson, Missouri, where she appears at the Charley Pride Theatre.

Stardom hasn't conflicted with Janie Fricke's strong Midwestern values. When she relaxes, she spends time with her family and her horses on a ranch in Texas. Thankful for her blessings, Janie feels that these values have helped her become the woman she is today. From Indiana farmgirl to internationally-acclaimed recording artist, she has never lost the pure heart and love of music that launched her career.

Texana Layered Mexican Dip
(Makes approximately 12 servings)

2 16-oz. cans refried beans (warm)
1/2 lb. cooked hamburger meat (warm)
1-1/2 c. grated cheese
2 6-oz. containers avocado dip
1 8-oz. carton sour cream

Spread all five (5) ingredients on a large platter in even
layers, in the order listed. If desired, garnish with
jalapeno peppers or Pico de Gallo and serve with warm
chips.

Green Chile Quiche
(Serves 8)

2 medium zucchini, shredded
   (squeeze out excess water)
2 finely chopped green onion
1/4 c. chopped green chile, canned
4 beaten egg whites
2 eggs or egg substitute
1 c. grated part skim mozzarella
1 c. grated cheddar cheese
1-1/2 c. evaporated skim milk
Vegetable coating spray

Saute squash and onion in non-stick skillet over low heat, until
tender. Add water if squash begins to stick. Mix all ingredients and
pour into 9-inch pan sprayed with vegetable coating spray. Bake at
350-degrees until firm and lightly browned. You may put into a pie
crust if you wish.

JENNIFER WILSON

This bubbly singer-dancer-actress-model is known as 'Branson's Morning Star' in the "live music capital of the world." Her Jennifer in the Morning show is a high-energy wake up call that showcases her vocal skills and phenomenal dancing abilities.

Born and raised in central Missouri, Jennifer began singing in church at the age of three; by age 16 she realized she wanted to dance professionally. Years of instruction has put those talented feet firmly on the stage of the Americana Theatre in Branson. "Branson has a wonderful asset," said Jennifer, "and that is its tremendous spirit."

ALMONDINE MANDARIN SALAD
(Serves 4-6)

4 tbsp. sugar, divided
1/2 cup slivered almonds
1/4 cup vegetable oil
2 tbsp. vinegar
1 tbsp. fresh parsley, minced
1/2 tsp. salt
1/8 tsp. pepper
1/8 tsp. hot pepper sauce
1 bunch fresh spinach, torn
1 can (11-oz.) mandarin oranges,
    drained
1 small red onion, sliced

Melt 3 tbsp. sugar over low heat; add almonds and stir until coated.

Cool and break into small pieces; set aside. In a jar with a tight-fitting lid, combine oil, vinegar, parsley, salt, pepper, hot pepper sauce and remaining sugar; shake well.

Just before serving, combine lettuce, oranges, onion and almonds in a large salad bowl. Shake dressing, pour over spinach and toss.

Triple Chocolate Malt Cookies
(Yields about 1-1/2 dozen)

1 cup butter-flavored shortening
1-1/4 cups brown sugar, packed
1/2 cup malted milk powder
2 tbsp. chocolate syrup
1 tbsp. vanilla extract
1 egg
2 cups flour
1 tsp. baking soda
1/2 tsp. salt
1-1/2 cups semi-sweet chocolate
    chunks
1 cup (6-oz.) milk chocolate chips
1/2 cup chopped pecans

Combine the first five ingredients; beat for two minutes then add egg.

Combine the flour, baking soda and salt; gradually add to creamed mixture, mixing well after each ingredient.

Stir in chocolate chunks, chips and pecans. Shape into 2-inch balls; place on ungreased baking sheets. Bake at 375 for 12-14 minutes or until golden brown. Cool for 2 minutes before removing to wire rack.

Fruits & Nut Dip
(Yields 2 cups)

1 8-oz. pkg. cream cheese, softened
1 tbsp. mayonnaise
1 7-oz. can pineapple, crushed
1/2 cup grapes, seedless
1 cup dates, chopped
1/2 cup pecans, chopped

Beat cream cheese and mayonnaise together. Stir in pineapple, grapes, dates and nuts. Cover and refrigerate for at least four hours. Serve with apple wedges. (Serving suggestions: use a dip for apple wedges, as spread for tea breads, Melba Toast, etc.)

JIM MABE

Jim Mabe claims that as a kid growing up in the Ozarks, he wasn't into being funny. Be that as it may, there is no doubt that as an adult he distilled every nuance of the complex art into a masterpiece of simplicity beloved by million of Baldknobber fans—the long-suffering, blank-faced Droopy Drawers.

Jim—with brothers Bill, Lyle and Bob and friend Chick Allen—banded together to form the Baldknobbers in the 1950s, performing at political rallies and parties after work and on weekends. Their first music show—often performed for less than a dozen people—opened on the waterfront of Lake Taneycomo. Now three generations of Mabes delight audiences in their 1,700-seat theatre on 76 Country Boulevard. And Jim may appear backwards on stage, but the man knows exactly what he's doing—on the stage, in the boardroom...and in the kitchen!

Mouth-Waterin' Catfish From Ole Droop Hisse'f

Jim's Blackened Catfish Fillets

1 Tbsp. paprika
Salt to taste
1 tsp. onion powder
1 tsp. garlic powder
1 tsp. cayenne pepper
3/4 tsp. white pepper

3/4 tsp. black pepper
1/2 tsp. thyme
4 catfish fillets
1/2 c. melted butter
lemon wedges

Preheat large heavy skillet until very hot. Combine first nine ingredients in a small bowl. Dip fillets in melted butter, then in seasoning mixture. Place in hot skillet, cook 2 - 3 minutes per side until blackened. Serve with squeeze of fresh lemon. Serves four.

Jim's Classic Fried Catfish with Hush Puppies

3/4 C. yellow cornmeal
1/4 C. flour
salt to taste
1 tsp. cayenne pepper

1/4 tsp. garlic powder
4 catfish fillets
vegetable oil

Combine first five ingredients. Coat catfish with mixture, shaking off excess. Fill deep pot half full with vegetable oil. Heat to 350 degrees F. Add catfish in a single layer and fry until golden brown, about 5 - 6 minutes. Remove and drain on paper towels. Serves four.

Jim's Hush Puppies

1 C. self-rising cornmeal
1/2 C. self-rising flour
1 Tbsp. sugar
1 egg

1 med. onion, chopped
1/2 green pepper, chopped
1 C. milk
vegetable oil

Combine first seven ingredients. Drop by tablespoons into hot vegetable oil (350 degrees). Fry until golden brown on all sides. Drain on paper towels.

JIM'S CATFISH FINGERS WITH THREE SAUCES

1/2 C. yellow cornmeal	1/3 C. milk
1 tsp. chili powder	1 egg
Salt to taste	vegetable oil
1/2 tsp. oregano	4 catfish fillets

In a bowl, combine first 4 ingredients. Beat together milk and egg. Cut catfish into thick sticks. Dip sticks into milk mixture, then in cornmeal. Heat oil to 350 degrees. Fry sticks in small batches, drain. Serve immediately with sauces. Serves 8.

Sauce suggestions: fresh or commercially prepared salsa, honey-mustard sauce or herb mayonnaise.

JIM'S CATFISH WITH MUSTARD-DILL SAUCE

4 catfish fillets	1 C. heavy cream
4 Tbsp. clarified butter	Dash hot pepper sauce
salt & pepper to taste	1 tsp. fresh lemon juice
2 Tbsp. shallots, finely chopped	2 tsp. fresh dill, minced
2 Tbsp. dry vermouth	lemon wedges
1 Tbsp. dijon mustard	

Heat butter in large skillet. Salt and pepper fillets to taste. Saute fillets for five minutes per side or until fish flakes easily. Remove to platter; keep warm. In same skillet, saute shallots until translucent. Add next five ingredients. Simmer until thick enough to coat a spoon. Add dill. Spoon circle of sauce on plate

JIM STAFFORD

Believe Jim Stafford's invitation when he says, "Let me entertain you!" He's a one-of-a-kind showman with an all-American grin, who captivates Branson audiences year-round with his special mix of wry humor and virtuoso musicianship.

The man who claims 'Branson' is an old Indian word for 'bumper-to-bumper,' Jim is also the person who blithely informs his audience, "Nah, all those cars are just Osmonds goin' to work." Jim describes Branson, the home of his 76 Country Boulevard theatre, as "a community of people who are all in competition with each other, but who all look after each other, somehow—a place where people still try to do the right thing."

Jim's wife's Ann, obviously knows how to feed him the right thing

Cow Patti's Cherry Congealed Salad

1 lg. can dark pitted cherries; save juice
8 oz. cream cheese
Small can of crushed pineapple, drained
Chopped pecans (I use almost a cup.)
16 oz. cold Coke
Lg. box of cherry gelatin

In a large glass baking dish combine half the cherries, the chopped nuts and the drained pineapple. Crumble the cream cheese into small bits and add. In a saucepan, take the juice from the cherries and bring to a boil. Add the large box of cherry gelatin and mix very well. Set aside to cool until mixture has thickened. Very slowly add the cold Coke to the mixture, then pour all over the stuff in the Pyrex dish.

Mix lightly with a fork. (You want the cream cheese to stay white, so don't stir too much). Cover with plastic wrap and chill. I usually make this the night before. Cut into squares and put on lettuce. Serves 12.

My Girl Bill's Shrimp in Sour Cream

1-1/2 lb. shrimp
2 C. sour cream
1/4 C. sherry
1/4 C. butter

2 green onions, minced
1/2 lb. mushrooms, sliced
2 Tbsp. flour
garlic salt and cayenne pepper to taste

Peel shrimp. Saute shrimp and onion in butter for 5 minutes until pink. Add mushrooms and cook 5 minutes longer. Blend in flour, salt, pepper, garlic salt, cayenne pepper. Add sour cream gradually and cook until thick. Doesn't take long, stirring constantly. Remove from heat and stir in sherry. Serve on whole wheat toast or cup forms.

Sweaty Betty's Sweet Potato Casserole

2 C. mashed sweet potatoes	1 C. milk
1-1/4 C. sugar	1/2 tsp. nutmeg
2 eggs beaten	1/2 tsp. cinnamon

Combine above ingredients in lightly greased baking dish and bake at 400° degrees for 20 minutes.

3/4 C. cornflakes	1/2 C. brown sugar
1/2 C. chopped nuts	3/4 C. stick melted butter

Combine and spread evenly over sweet potato mixture. Bake 10 more minutes.

Jim Stafford's, Earn as You Learn Texas Beans

1 (16 oz.) pkg. dried pinto beans	lemon pepper
1/2 to 1 tsp. cayenne	seasoned salt
pepper to taste	1 lg. hamhock
1 tsp. garlic	1 lb. lean hamburger
2 bay leaves	1 onion, chopped

Soak beans in water overnight. Cover with water, add seasonings and hamhock and cook until tender. Cook hamburger and chopped onion in separate skillet. Add to beans. Remember, this is "Earn as You Learn" – try seasonings to your taste!

Black Water Hattie's Blackeye Pie Jambalaya

1 lg. onion, chopped	4 cups rice
1 bell pepper, chopped	2 pods garlic, minced
1 lb. ham, sausage, chicken, bacon or combination thereof, cubed	
2 Tbsp. bacon grease	3 bay leaves
2 (15 oz.) cans black eyed peas	salt and red pepper
1 jalapeno pepper, seeded and minced	

Saute onion, bell pepper, and garlic in bacon grease. After 10 minutes, add black-eye peas, jalapeno pepper, bay leaves and simmer one-half hour. In a separate pot, cook rice according to the directions, but add your choice of meats to the rice pot while cooking. When rice is done, combine the beans and rice, add seasoning and serve.

Kirby VanBurch, "Prince of Magic

Kirby VanBurch, who has traveled the world with a spectacular showcase of grand illusions and his exotic menagerie, received his first magic kit at age seven. "I discovered magic as a child...a time when you still don't know your limitations. I've never let go of that."

His first tiger was a gift from an uncle...and his family of exotic animals has grown from there. Kirby's been known to say with a laugh, "The only person who's had more animals in his show was Noah."

Co-starring with comedian Philip Wellford at Branson's Magical Mansion, Kirby insists the 'magic' of Branson isn't its music shows. "It's about real people, friendliness, family and God. Branson is a magnet for what America used to be, and it's an honor to perform for people who share the same values."

Kirby's Safari Shrimp

1-1/2 cups onion, chopped
1 cup celery, finely chopped
2 medium green peppers, chopped
2 cloves garlic, minced
1/4 cup butter
1 can (15-oz.) tomato sauce
1 cup water
2 tsp. parsley, snipped
1 tsp. salt
1/8 tsp. cayenne red pepper
2 bay leaves, crushed
14 to 16 oz. shrimp, fresh or
    frozen raw, cleaned shrimp
3 cups rice, cooked

Cook and stir onion, celery, green pepper and garlic in butter until onion is tender. Remove from heat; stir in tomato sauce, water and seasonings. Simmer uncovered 10 minutes. Add water if need. Stir in shrimp; heat to boiling. Cover and cook over medium heat 10 to 20 minutes. Serve over rice.

JUNGLE GUMBO
(Serves 8 to 10)

2 lb. peeled shrimp
1 lb. crab meat
1/3 cup flour
1/3 cup liquid veg. oil
2 cups onion, chopped
2 cups celery, chopped
1 cup bell pepper, chopped
1 pkg. (10-oz.) frozen, cut okra
1 8-oz. can tomato sauce
1/4 cup fresh parsley, chopped
1 13-oz. can chicken broth
3 bay leaves
2 tbsp. Worcestershire sauce
1 tbsp. thyme
1 tbsp. Kitchen Bouquet
2 tsps. garlic
Salt & pepper to taste
Liquid hot pepper to taste
Hot, cooked rice

To make roux, heat oil in large cast iron kettle, if available. When very hot, but not smoking, add half the flour, stirring constantly with a wire whisk. Add remaining flour. Stir rapidly with whisk until dark and smooth.

Add vegetables and cook until tender. Add tomato sauce, 2 cups water and chicken broth. Simmer for 1 hour. Add remaining ingredients, except rice. Simmer for 15 minutes. Serve over hot rice.

THE LENNON SISTERS

Janet, Kathy, Peggy and Dee Dee

The Lennon Sisters are an American Institution—this country fell in love with them as the definitive "girls next door." For 13 years, on the Lawrence Welk Show, they charmed the nation with their sweet-voiced harmonies. The combination of their extraordinary natural vocal talents, hard working professionalism, striking looks, unassuming personalities and strong family values has earned them a place in the hearts of millions of fans nationwide.

Now, the girls next door *are* next door! In 1994 they moved—lock, stock and barrel—to Branson, to become the featured performers at the Welk Champagne Theatre.

...et, Kathy, Peggy and Dee Dee, Right, prove too many cooks couldn't spoil the Lennons' broth.

Dee Dee Lennon

ONE-PAN POTATOES AND CHICKEN ROSEMARY
(Serves 4)

4 med. potatoes	2 cloves garlic, minced
1 lb. chicken breasts,	2 tbsp. olive oil
boned and skinned	2 tsp. dried rosemary, crumbled

Slice potatoes 1/4-inch thick and microwave until tender, 8 to 10 minutes. Place garlic and olive oil in large skillet, heat to medium-high. Cut chicken into 1/2-inch strips, add to skillet and brown for 5 minutes. Add potatoes and rosemary, saute and toss until potatoes are lightly browned. Season with salt and pepper. (Time: 20 minutes!)

Janet Lennon

STUFFED POTATO PUFFS
(Serves 4)

3 large baking potatoes, scrubbed	2 tbsp. brandy (or white wine)
1/2 lb. fresh mushrooms	1/2 tsp. fresh ground pepper
Vegetable cooking spray oil	1 tbsp. minced garlic
1 tsp. butter	2 tbsp. green onion, minced
1/2 cup Parmesan cheese,	1/4 tsp. salt
freshly grated	

Cook potatoes in a large saucepan, covered in boiling water, for 50 minutes or until tender. Drain and let cool. Remove stems and chop mushroom caps; set aside. Coat a large non-stick skillet with cooking spray, add butter and place over medium heat; add garlic and saute 2 minutes. Stir in chopped mushrooms, cover and reduce heat, and cook 6 minutes or until tender, stirring occasionally. Stir in brandy (or wine) and pepper and cook uncovered until liquid evaporates. Remove from heat and cool.

Peel and mash potatoes. Stir in minced green onion and salt. Line a baking sheet with waxed paper and spoon 1/4 cup potato mixture in a 3 inch circle—repeat with remaining potato to form 16 circles.

Spoon mushroom mixture evenly into the center of 8 circles. Top with remaining circles and press gently around edges to seal. Pinch edges of each side to form star shape. Sprinkle top with cheese and place stuffed potato patties on baking sheet coated with cooking spray. Bake at 400 for 25 minutes or until golden. To serve, place 2 puffs on each serving plate.

Kathy Lennon

POLYNESIAN PORK
(Serves 4)

1 lb. (a little more won't hurt!)
   pork tenderloin or chops
2 tbsp. margarine or oil
1 can pineapple chunks
1/4 cup bottled Russian dressing
3/4 tbsp. soy sauce
1/2 tsp. vinegar

1/8 tsp. salt
2/3 cup water
1-1/4 tbsp. cornstarch
1/4 of a green pepper
   thinly sliced
1 onion, chopped
Rice or Chinese noodles

Fry pork in oil until brown; drain off fat. Mix pineapple juice with next four ingredients. Stir in water which has been mixed with cornstarch. Pour over meat and simmer 30 minutes. Add green pepper, onion and pineapple. Simmer 15 minutes (no more!). Green pepper should be sorta crisp. Serve over rice.

(We don't like the pineapple in the pork, so I just use the juice from the can and put fruit in salad to go with the dish—bananas and pineapple, mixed with mayonnaise, on lettuce.)

Peggy Lennon

MANICOTTI

3 cups of your favorite
   spaghetti sauce, heated
1 box manicotti noodles
   (10-12)

Filling:
2 cartons Ricotta cheese
   (2 cups, approx.)
1-1/2 cups Mozzarella, grated
1 cup Parmesan
1 tbsp. sugar
1 egg
1 to 2 tbsp. parsley

Mix filling thoroughly, then stuff into uncooked noodles using a table knife. Pour 1 cup heated spaghetti sauce into bottom of 9"x13" glass pan. Place noodles side by side in pan. Pour remaining, heated sauce over all, seal tightly with aluminum foil and let stand at least 2 hours.

Bake at 400 for approximately 50 minutes. Take off foil, sprinkle with more Parmesan and bake another 10-15 minutes.

LOUISE MANDRELL

Louise Mandrell joined her sister Barbara's band, the Do-Rites, when she was 15 years old, and toured with the group for several years. From there she went on to Grand Ole Opry star Stu Phillip's group, and then sang lead and back-up for Merle Haggard before striking out on her own.

Appearances on the Mandrell's hit television series brought Louise more fame—and more performances. As time went by, more and more of those performances were in Branson, at Roy Clark's Celebrity Theatre and the Lowe's. When the Grand Palace opened, Louise and Glen Campbell were named co-hosts for the season—in 1994, she brought her hit song-and-dance production, "Love My Country" to town.

Constantly working to improve her performance, Louise always gives 100%—and loves every minute of it!

Louise's Bacon-Cheese-Tomato Pie

Pastry for 8" - 9", 2 crust pie (Pillsbury all ready pie crusts)

8 oz. bacon, fried
4 tomatoes, sliced
(peeled if you like)
6 oz. shredded mozzarella cheese
1 Tbsp. milk

2/3 C. each onion & green bell
pepper, chopped
6 oz. shredded cheddar cheese
Tabasco

Line pie plate with half of pastry (one circle) and prick bottom.

Break bacon into large pieces and place half of pieces on bottom of pie shell; cover with 1/3 cup each of onion and bell pepper. Cover with 1/2 of tomato slices; sprinkle with Tabasco. Next, cover with cheddar cheese. Repeat these layers starting with remaining bacon and finishing with mozzarella cheese. Place remaining pastry circle on top, dampening edge of pastry and pressing edges together. Make several slits on top, and decorate with pastry leaves made from trimmings if you like. Glaze with the milk, and bake for 35 minutes.

When serving, if there is a lot of juice on the bottom of the pie, just drain after you've cut and removed your first slice. This dish is excellent in the summer when made with homegrown tomatoes and bell peppers.

Louise 's Peanut Butter Jumbos

1-1/2 C. butter
1-1/2 C. granulated sugar
3 eggs
1-1/2 tsp. baking soda

1-1/2 C. peanut butter
1-1/2 C. brown sugar
3 C. all purpose flour
1 pkg. Reeses peanut butter chips

Beat together butter, peanut butter and sugars until light and fluffy; blend in eggs.

Combine flour and soda; blend into peanut butter mixture. Stir in chips. Drop dough by level 1/4 cup measures onto greased cookie sheets 3" apart.

Bake in 350° oven for 12-14 minutes. Cool cookies on sheet for 3 minutes, remove to wire rack until cool. Yields: 3 dozen.

Louise's Chicken and Dressing Casserole

Ingredients:

4 lb. whole chicken
3 stalks of celery
1-1/2 tsp. salt
1 can cream of mushroom soup
1 (12 oz.) can evaporated milk
1/3 C. melted butter

1 - 2 onions
1 small carrot
1 can cream of chicken soup
1/4 C. cooking sherry
1 pkg. Pepperidge Farm herb
    stuffing mix

Put chicken and vegetables in large pot and cover with with water. Add salt and bring to a boil. Cover and reduce to low. Cook 1 to 1-1/2 hours, until tender. Remove chicken to cool; debone and tear into small pieces. In food processor, puree onion, celery and carrot with 1 cup of cooled broth.

In another saucepan, mix soups, sherry, milk and pureed broth from the food processor together, heat slowly until warmed.

In a bowl, mix together stuffing and butter. Now we can begin to assemble casserole.

In a large 13" x 9" x 2" pyrex baking dish which has been sprayed with Pam, pour 1 cup of soup mixture. Next sprinkle 1/2 of stuffing/butter mixture evenly over soup. Next, layer 1/2 of the chicken pieces and 1/2 of the remaining soup mixture. Repeat these layers starting again with the stuffing mix, then remaining chicken, and remaining soup. (Optional), finish by topping casserole with 3 or 4 oz. package of slivered almonds or cashews.

Bake for 30 minutes or until bubbly in 325° oven. Serve with lots of cranberry sauce!

Delicious! Serves: 8

LOWE SISTERS

Branson entertainment pioneers, the Lowe Sisters, have returned to the footlights. The dynamic singers can be found performing lunch and dinner shows at their new venue—on Hwy. 165 —called Branson Town. "We were the ones that started coming out with the national artists," said sister Teresa Lowe, about her family's historical contributions to the Branson phenomena. "And we're not afraid of newness, and we're going to give it our best shot.

It'll come as no surprise that these great vocalists are also great cooks. Try lunch...Lowe style!

AUTOGRAPH
_____

AUTOGRAPH
_____

AUTOGRAPH
_____

AUTOGRAPH
_____

Family Favorites From
Sheila Lowe-Weeks

SWEET POTATO CASSEROLE

3 C. cooked mashed sweet potatoes	1/2 C. butter, softened
1 C. granulated sugar	1 C. firmly packed brown sugar
2 eggs, lightly beaten	1/3 C. all purpose flour
1 tsp. vanilla	1/3 C. butter
1/3 C. milk	1 C. finely chopped pecans

Combine in bowl with electric mixer or good processor: sweet potatoes, granulated sugar, eggs, vanilla, milk and 1/2 cup butter. Beat until smooth. Spoon into a greased 2-quart shallow casserole dish.

In another bowl combine brown sugar, flour, 1/3 cup butter and pecans. Sprinkle mixture over top of sweet potato mixture.

Bake in 350° degree oven 45 minutes, or until topping is lightly browned and bubbly.

SOUTHERN BISCUITS

1 pkg. yeast (or 1 cake)	1 C. vegetable shortening
1/4 C. warm water	3 - 4 C. self-rising flour
5 Tbsp. granulated sugar	2 C. buttermilk

Soften yeast in warm water. Add sugar. Stir in shortening, flour and buttermilk until just moistened. Kneed dough lightly on floured surface. Cut with 2-inch biscuit cutter and place on ungreased cookie sheet. Bake in 450° degree oven 20-25 minutes or until lightly browned.

This recipe will keep for a week in the refrigerator stored in a tight container.

Heavenly Chocolate Pie

2 tsp. butter
3 Tbsp. cocoa
1/3 C. all purpose flour
1 C. granulated sugar
2-1/2 C. milk

3/4 C. vanilla
1/4 tsp. salt
3 eggs yolks
Baked pastry crust or
    graham cracker crust

In saucepan, melt butter. Add cocoa, flour, 1 C. sugar, milk, vanilla, salt and egg yolks. Stir constantly until mixture comes to a boil. Cool slightly, then pour into baked pastry crust or graham cracker crust. Top with meringue. Bake in 400° degree oven 5 minutes, or until meringue is lightly browned. Cool thoroughly before serving.

Meringue

3 egg whites,
    at room temperature

1/4 C. granulated sugar
1/2 tsp. vanilla

In chilled mixing bowl beat egg whites until they form soft peaks. Slowly add 1/4 C. sugar and vanilla. Continue beating at high speed until stiff peaks form. Spread meringue over pie.

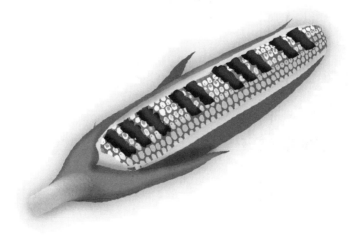

MAGGIE LaMEE

Known in these-here-hills as 'Rhetta Cupp,' one of Pump Boys and Dinettes beloved Cupp sisters, Maggie LaMee is also an accomplished jingle singer who may have enticed you to fly United, eat at McDonalds or drive an Oldsmobile.

She has had a long association with Pump Boys and Dinettes, performing the role of Rhetta Cupp on Broadway, in Los Angeles, Houston, and in the acclaimed Chicago production. She has directed the show at the Kennedy Center for the Performing Arts in Washington, DC, in Alaska, Texas, Ohio, St. Louis, and Santa Fe.

Maggie is also one of the five producers responsible for bringing Pump Boys and Dinettes to a permanent home in Branson.

DINETTES DOWN-HOME DELICIOUS MEATLOAF
Serves a family of 4 or 5

5 lbs. ground beef	1/2 tbsp. pepper
1-1/4 cup bread crumbs	1 tbsp. garlic salt
1 cup milk	1/2 cup diced onion
1/2 barbecue sauce	1 egg
1 tbsp. salt	1 cup Monterey Jack

Mix all ingredients and bake at 350 for 45 minutes.

MAGGIE'S ALL-TIME FAVORITE PASTA

Chop up into chunky pieces (1 cup each):Zucchini, Mushrooms, Red onion, Broccoli Place veggies in bowl and toss with with:
4 crushed cloves garlic, 1/2 cup balsamic vinegar, 2 tbsp. olive oil
Crushed red pepper, basil and black pepper (to taste)

Maggie LaMee is featured on the right.

MEL TILLIS

There's not a star in Branson more comfortable in front of a kitchen stove—not to mention a crowd—than Mel Tillis. What he didn't learn about cooking from his dad, who owned a bakery in Pahokee, Florida, the U.S. Air Force was happy to teach him when he enlisted in 1951.

"When I took the (U.S.A.F.) aptitude test, I didn't tell them that I was a cook or a baker. And I'll be dog-goned if that aptitude didn't say I was a baker! So I served my country all right... I served 'em cakes, cookies, pies, and doughnuts!"

M-M-Mel is a talented cook, an inspired gardener and a legendary entertainer. At his 2,100-seat theatre he combines all the loves of his life—with a stage at one end and his family and kitchen on the other.

Mel's Country Summer Day Dinner

6 center cut pork chops
6 med. turnips and greens
potato salad
beets

cornbread
green onions
blackberry cobbler

Greens

First: Stem Greens and pick out old or tough leaves. Wash greens thoroughly three times. Remove all the dirt and bugs and all the other little critters. "The dirt and grit causes kidney stones and gall stones," so Mama says to wash the greens three times, and if you didn't she'd get you!

Now, after you've picked and stemmed and washed the greens real good, put them in a large cooking pot. Peel and slice the turnips into 1/4 in. chips, and layer them along with the six porkchops in with the greens. Mama says, "The secret to good greens is 1 tsp. of sugar and NO salt at all." Mama lets you salt your own.

Put about two cups of water into the pot. The water keeps the greens from burning, and the steam helps wilt the greens down to start cooking in their own juices.

Next: Slice off about 10 pieces of white bacon and place the pieces in a skillet and cook until all the fat has rendered out of the bacon. Pour hot bacon grease over the greens. Put the bacon on a plate to be served at meal time also. Cover pot with a lid and cook greens on high until water starts to boil, then turn down the heat to low. Mama says, "It takes about 45 minutes to 1 hour to make good greens." It depends on how tender you want them. Don't you take that lid off until they're done, 'les you want to get your hand slapped!

Green Onions

While the greens and pork chops are cooking and making "Pot Licker," clean and wash two bunches of green onions. Cut the tops off about half way down; then put them in a large drinking glass filled with cold water. Wrap the tops that are sticking out with plastic wrap and put them in the refrigerator. When the greens are ready to serve, the onions will be cold, crisp and good!

Potato Salad

Put 6 medium Idaho potatoes (or any ole tater will do) peeled, washed and diced into 1 in. cubes into a pot and cover with water. Put 5 eggs in the same pot and bring to a boil. Cover with a lid and turn down low. Mama says, "Cooking the eggs in the same pot with the potatoes saves electricity or stove wood." Makes sense to me! Mama was always real conservative. She had to be.

While that's cooking combine in a large bowl: 2 med. onions, diced; 1/2 bell pepper, diced; 6 lg. sweet pickles, diced; 1 sm. jar pimentos, diced; 1 stalk celery, diced; 4 Tbsp. salad dressing (Miracle Whip); 3 Tbsp. mustard.

When the eggs are hard boiled and the taters are done, take the eggs out and let them cool down a bit 'fore you peel them, else you'll be peeling and a juggling at the same time.

After you've peeled the eggs, slice them into 1/4 in. chips and mix them and potatoes and all the other ingredients together. Don't over mix, but make sure you have a good blend. Cover with plastic wrap and put into refrigerator. It'll be just right when the meal is served.

Beets

Put a jar or can of beets in the refrigerator about four or five hours before the meal is served. No, don't forget to put them on the table at meal time, (I sometimes do). But when I do remember them, there's nothing better to eat with greens and that browned white bacon you fried than cold beets.

Corn Bread (from Scratch!)

1 Teflon skillet with lid
2 Tbsp. plain flour
1 tsp. salt

2 C. plain corn meal
2 tsp. baking powder
1 tsp. baking soda

Combine these ingredients and mix thoroughly until all lumps are out.
1/4 C cooking oil
1 egg
2 C. buttermilk

Combine and mix thoroughly. Preheat Teflon skillet on high til hot. Combine all ingredients in mixing bowl and mix 'til all ingredients are blended well. Pour into hot skillet and shake around until the batter is level. Put a lid on the skillet and turn burner down to low and let cornbread cook until done. (about20 min.) When done, turn cornbread over with an egg turner and let it brown on the other side. Don't put lid back on skillet while other side browns.

Blackberry Cobbler

Preheat oven to 425 degrees
Combine and mix:
2 C. sugar

2 C. self rising flour
2 C. milk

Butter a large glass baking dish and set in oven to preheat. When dish is hot, pour combined ingredients into dish. Sprinkle 2 C. blackberries into baking dish over combined ingredients. Bake at 425 degrees until golden brown on top. Sprinkle sugar on top of pie while pie is still hot. Serve with fresh cream.

*Serve with iced tea,
bread and butter pickles,
pickled hot pepper sauce
(to pour over greens),
and apple sauce.
Mama says,
"Serve apple sauce to help
digest the pork chops,
else you'll get trichinosis,"
whatever that is!*

God Bless The Cook
And Thank You!
Mel Tillis

MICKEY GILLEY

Decades of people have figured out that if Mickey Gilley's name is on it, a good time can't be far behind. Rock 'n' roll and country fans of the 60s and 70s knew it—honky-tonkers in Houston's "Gilley's Club" in the 80s were absolutely certain of it.

And whether Branson's 1990s visitors are in one of his theatre seats or in a booth at his "Texas Cafe," this great Gilley tradition continues.

Mickey says it would be enjoyable to be sitting in Branson in a motorhome, enjoying all the shows—but he'd rather be on stage entertaining his audience. "I believe that as long as I give an honest performance, the fans will support me," he said. "I plan to be a part of Branson for a long time."

Mickey Gilley – "Favorite Recipes" Taken From My Cookbook

COUNTRY FRIED PORK CHOPS
(Mickey's Favorite)

Big center cut chops (not too thin). Salt and pepper well on both sides. Drop in hot deep Crisco oil. Lower fire and cook well until brown. Turn on both sides.

Great with hot biscuits.

COUNTRY STYLE HAM SLICE

1 center slice ham 2" thick
1 tsp. dry mustard

1 C brown sugar
1-1/4 C pineapple juice

Mix 3/4 cup brown sugar with mustard in small bowl. Rub both sides of ham with mixture. Place ham in baking dish. Sprinkle with remaining sugar, add pineapple juice and bake at 350 degrees for 2 hours until tender.

BAKED HAM

16 - 20 lb. ham
1-1/2 C water
1 can cherries
2 tbsp. brown sugar

1 lg. can sliced pineapple
2 (16 oz.) Cokes
1 small jar honey

Remove excess fat from ham. Rub honey all over ham. Pour water and Coke in bottom of pan. Place in oven at 350° for 2 hours, basting occasionally. When cool, rub with brown sugar. Place pineapple rings and cherries on top with toothpicks. Cover with foil and bake another hour.

Country Fried Chicken

| 1 fryer cut up | 1 C flour | Salt and pepper |

Cut up chicken, wash and drain. Salt and pepper all over. Roll into flour until well coated. Fry in deep Crisco until golden brown.

Homemade Biscuits

| Self-rising flour (Pillsbury) | 1 Tbsp. Crisco oil |
| 1 C buttermilk | 1/2 tsp. baking soda |

Make a well in round pan or skillet. Work flour in with oil and buttermilk until dough is hard enough to knead. Roll out and cut and bake about 15 minutes at 500°. This makes about 1 dozen.

Chicken In Red Gravy With Green Peas

1 chicken cup up	1 lg. onion
1 lg. bell pepper	1 clove garlic
2 (8 oz.) cans tomato sauce	1 lg. can green peas
1/4 C oil	2 Tbsp. flour
Salt and pepper to taste	

Brown chicken in large heavy pot with cover. Remove chicken, add flour and brown, then saute onion and bell pepper. Add 2 cans sauce and garlic. Drain green peas and add to gravy. Replace chicken to mixture and simmer 45 minutes on low heat.

Fresh Country String Beans

1-1/2 lb. fresh string beans
2 Tbsp. oil
1 small piece salt pork

Snap beans and wash well. Cover well with water. Add salt pork and oil. Bacon grease can be used. Cover and cook on low heat until beans are tender. Check to be sure all the water has not cooked out. No salt should be added.

MIKE ITO

During a winter tour in 1979, the Baldknobbers found Mike Ito in Dallas, where he was entertaining at Willie Nelson's place with the "Side of the Road Gang." They invited him and his smokin' country fiddle to join them on their Branson stage—a place the spotlights still find him in to this day.

Country music hooked this Toyko, Japan native as a young boy. The world of entertainment had snared him much sooner—it was a family affair. Mike's mom designs costumes, and his dad is a movie designer who has won the Japanese equivalent of an "Oscar" for his talent.

This great cook and talented musician's ambition is to keep on making great country music on the Baldknobbers stage...and to keep on making those "pot stickers" in the kitchen!

A Baldknobber Who Likes
To "Fiddle" In The Kitchen

SUKIYAKI

Ingredients (4 servings)
1-1/2 lbs. beef tenderloin
2 oz. Shirataki`
1 piece broiled Tofu
4 eggs

A
1/3 cup plus 1 Tbsp. MIRIN
1/3 cup plus 1 Tbsp. soy sauce
1/3 cup plus 1 Tbsp. broth
5 Tbsp. sugar
A Jino Moto

1. Cut beef into thin slices. Cut green onions on the bias. Wash and boil shirataki or vermicelli. Drain and cut. Cut broiled tofu in 8 pieces.

2. Make mixture A (warishita) and set aside.

3. Arrange meat attractively on a large plate, placing a few pieces of sliced beef suet in the center like a rose bud. Arrange vegetables on another plate.

4. Preheat skillet, add suet and rub over bottom and sides to grease. Add beef and vegetables little at a time.

5. Just before eating, dip meat and vegetables in beaten raw egg in small individual bowls.

Note:

• In order to maintain the delicate flavor, do not cook beef and vegetable all at once.

• Mushrooms and burdocks are also tasty.

• A thick frying pan may be used, instead of a skillet.

In Japan, during the period of strong Buddhist influence, the eating of meat was prohibited. The few people who recognized the nutritional value of meat, were compelled to eat it secretly. At that time it was commonly broiled on a farming tool called SUKI (spade). Hence the name SUKIYAKI. It is probably one of the most internationally known Japanese dishes.

Gyoza (Pot Stickers)
(2 *servings*)

1/2 cup round onion, diced
20 round shape egg roll skin
1/2 lb. ground pork
1/2 cup cabbage, diced
1/4 cup green onion, diced

1 egg
3 cloves garlic, diced
1/4 tsp. salt
1/4 tsp. pepper

1) Mix all and wrap with egg roll skin.
2) Bake with frying pan until one side is brown
3) Add 1/2 cup of water and lid until all water is gone with high heat

Sauce:
    1 Tbsp. sesame oil
    2 Tbsp. soy sauce

    3 Tbsp.rice vinegar
    1/2 tsp. red pepper

Tempura
(4 *servings*)

tempura batter

12 medium sized prawns
11 oz. of white meat fish fillet
1 large bunch of parsley
1/2 sheet nori
1 cup grated radish
2 Tbsp. grated ginger root

1 egg
1-1/2 cups ice cold water
2-1/4 cups flour
Frying Oil
Tempura sauce
    1-1/5 cups broth
    5 Tbsp. soy sauce
    3-1/2 Tbsp. mirin
    A Jino Moto

    1. Remove the head and shell of the prawns, leaving the tails on. Slit the front with a knife in order to prevent shrinking in oil. Wash and cut parsley. Cut a NORI sheet into four rectangles.

    2. Beat eggs well, pour in ice cold water and sift in flour. Blend lightly.

    3. Dip fresh ingredients in batter. Heat oil to 350°F – 370°F and put ingredients in near the brim of pan, stirring with chopsticks. Fry well on both sides. Fry parsley and NORI sheets with less batter. Drain and place on a sheet of Japanese paper.

    4. Make TEMPURA sauce. Serve with grated radish and ginger root in TEMPURA sauce.

    Variation: Vegetable tempura. Fried vegetables with TEMPURA batter– burdock, carrot, lotus root and string beans, etc.

THE OSMOND FAMILY
Merrill, Jimmy, Jay, Wayne & Alan

The Osmond's singing career began in their native Ogden, Utah church. But it was an appearance on "Disneyland After Dark"—a segment seen by Andy Williams' father—that really launched them into the "Big Time." Although the entertainer usually gets credit for 'discovering' the Osmonds, Williams said his father caught the show and hauled the boys into rehearsal one day. "(My father) made us all stop what we were doing...and they got up and sang. They had it all, and they were really funny. They knocked everybody out... and the rest is history."

The Osmonds were among the best and most popular acts of the 1970s. And Alan, Wayne, Merrill, Jay and Donny weren't the only Osmonds topping the charts—Jimmy recorded his first album in Japanese and scored the Osmonds first gold record.

The legendary family has found no boundaries for their diverse talents. "Only in America," Jimmy declares, "could a family such as our have the opportunity to work together for 36 years and still be going strong in the music business. And it is for that reason—from family harmonies to family values—that we find ourselves here in Branson."

AUTOGRAPH

AUTOGRAPH

AUTOGRAPH

AUTOGRAPH

Olive Osmond's Favorite Recipe:

How To Preserve a Husband

Be careful in your selection. Do not choose too young. When selected, give your entire thoughts to preparation for domestic use. Some wives insist upon keeping them in a pickle; others are constantly getting them into hot water. This may make them sour, hard and sometimes bitter—even poor varieties may be made sweet, tender and good by garnishing them with patience, well-sweetened with love and seasoned with kisses. Wrap them in a mantle of charity. Keep warm with a steady fire of domestic devotion and serve with peaches and cream. Thus prepared, they will keep for years. (Author unknown)

Jimmy's Favorite Chinese Chicken Salad

6 chicken breasts,
   deboned & skinned
Kikkoman Teriyaki Sauce

Dressing:
3/4 c. salad oil
1/2 c. Japanese rice vinegar
2 tsp. salt
1 tbsp. sesame oil
1/3 c. sugar
1 tsp. pepper

Bake in sauce in 300-degree oven for 30 minutes, turn over and bake an additional 30 minutes. Cool and cut into cubes. Put cubes in marinade overnight—or at least 2 hours.

Make up salad of iceberg, romaine or red leaf lettuce. Add sliced onion, 1/4 c. slivered almonds and 1/4 c. sesame seeds. Add chicken cubes to salad and garnish with wonton (but wonton skins into strips and cook in peanut oil). Toss in dressing and serve.

Jay's Carrot Cake

Combine:
3 c. grated raw carrots
1-1/2 c. oil
4 eggs
2 c. sugar

In another bowl mix:
2 c. flour
3 tsp. baking soda
2 tsp. cinnamon
1 tsp. salt

Blend together, then add 1/2 c. nuts. Bake at 350-degrees for 45 minutes, cool and frost with cream cheese frosting.

Merrill's Favorite Salad

Cook, drain and chill:
Shell macaroni

Add:
lettuce, chopped
celery, diced
cucumbers, diced
green onions, diced
pimentos, cut into small pieces
tuna fish, large can
green peppers, diced

Toss together with:
Mayonnaise thinned with evaporated milk and seasoned with garlic salt and a bit of sugar. Note: other things may be added as desired, such as crab meat, olives, capers, shrimp, etc.

Jay's "Einstein" Salad

(Note from Olive: "When Jay was small, he objected to bean sprouts and wanted to know why I put them in the salad. I told him it was because they had "enzymes" in them and they were good for us to eat. That evening at dinner, he said, "Please pass the Einstein Salad.' We have called it that ever since."

Toss with your favorite dressing: lettuce, celery, cucumbers, carrots, turnips, radishes, bean sprouts...

PHILIP WELLFORD

P hilip Wellford won't cook a squash—but he'll juggle one in a heartbeat. (The man just won't stop playing with his food...)

Raised in Sarasota, Florida, the former winter quarters for the Ringling, Barnum and Bailey Circus, Philip Wellford jokingly reminisces that, as a child, he always dreamed of one day running away from the circus to join a home. Ironically, he was in graduate school before he discovered a hidden talent— juggling—which put him on the road with the Royal Liechtenstein Circus.

The Emmy award-winning comedian now co-headlines in the VanBurch and Wellford Show at Branson's Magical Mansion (formerly the Shenandoah). This popular show juggles a spicy mix of Philip's humor and illusionist Kirby VanBurch's magic that is guaranteed to satisfy everyone's entertainment appetite.

Philip's Chicken-To-Die-For

Step One:
Dust two 4-oz. chicken breasts in one cup seasoned flour

Step Two:
Cook chicken breasts in fry pan until golden brown, in 1-oz. Olive oil. Drain chicken on paper towel.

Step Three:
Whip 1 qt. Half and Half with six egg yolks.

Step Four:
In sauce pan add:
    1/2 tsp. fresh garlic (or 4 cloves)
    1/2-oz. white wine
    1-oz. olive oil
Cook ingredients together (brown but don't burn garlic).

Drain and add:
    1/3 cup artichokes
    1/8 cup fresh mushrooms
    1/8 cup roasted red pepper

Mix all ingredients in sauce pan; add chicken breasts, and warm all the ingredients.

Slowly add 1/2 cup freshly grated Parmesan cheese to thicken sauce.

Blanch 6-oz. Fettuccine Noodles. Serve chicken breast on top of noodles. Pour remaining ingredients over chicken.

Dust with parsley and enjoy!

RAY STEVENS

I f laughter was the coin of the realm, the richest man in country-America would be Ray Stevens. On the radio or in person, Ray has piled up more giggles, snickers, chortles and chuckles with his definitively wacky songs than anyone could count.

Ahab the Arab, *Gitarzan* and *The Streak* are just the tips of the entertainment iceberg for this multi-talented entertainer. Ray is one of the most-awarded musicians, songwriters, singers, arrangers and comedians in the country.

His presence in the theatre scene here contributed to the explosive phenomena that became live entertainment's largest legend— Branson. And the red carpet is always rolled out when Ray rolls back to town.

Ray Stevens – A Comedian Cookin' At His Corner Of Branson!

RAYMONE'S SALAD

1/2 head Iceberg lettuce	1/2 head Romaine lettuce
3 small onions	1 bell pepper
1 small can artichoke hearts (drain)	1 small can asparagus tips
(4 or 5 small hearts, drain)	4 radishes
1 large tomato	1 carrot
2 large celery stems	2 hard boiled eggs
1 C. cottage cheese	sweet pickles
India relish	bacon bits

Chop and mix above ingredients.
Mix together the following and add to above mixture:
   2 Tbsp. avocado dressing
   2 Tbsp. blue cheese dressing
   2 Tbsp. 1000 Island dressing

RAYMONE'S BEANIE WEENIES

1 med. size onion	1 med. size green bell pepper
2 celery sticks (10-inches each)	1/2 lb. ground beef
1 pkg. wieners	1 lg. can baked beans (55 oz.)
1 C. brown sugar	Tobasco (15 dashes, or to taste)

Dice and saute the onion, green pepper and celery in butter until the onions look slightly opaque. Transfer this mixture to a large pot and set aside.

Crumble and brown ground beef, drain grease and transfer to the large pot also.

Drain baked beans, remove any pork fat and add to large pot.

Cut wieners into bite-size pieces and add to pot. Stir in brown sugar. Add Tobasco. Heat thoroughly over low temperature and serve.

ROY CLARK

Mix well: Roy Clark's astounding musical ability, his quick wit, adorable smile and genuine love for people...and you have the recipe for one of American music's best entertainers.

The first major country star to establish a permanent venue in Branson (in 1983), Roy's still pickin' and grinnin' his way through a high-profile career. And a high-voltage show—a winning combination of variety music and "Hee-Haw" revisited that delights audiences—that plays over 200 times a year at the Roy Clark Celebrity Theatre.

Calling Branson "a town that cares about the people who come here," Roy laughs when asked about retirement. "I'm not going to retire. As long as my audience lasts and we can grow old together, I'll just fade into an encore in heaven!"

Roy's Biscuits

1 pkg. dry yeast
2 Tbsp. warm water (105°-115°)
2 C. buttermilk
5 C. all-purpose flour
1 tsp. salt

Sugar substitute to equal
 1/4 cup sugar
1 Tbsp. baking powder
1 tsp. soda
1 C. shortening

Steps in preparation:
1. Combine yeast and warm water; let stand 5 minutes or until bubbly.
2. Add buttermilk to yeast mixture, and set aside.
3. Combine dry ingredients in large bowl; cut in shortening until mixture resembles coarse crumbs.
4. Add buttermilk mixture to dry mixture, stirring with fork until dry ingredients are moistened.
5. Turn dough out on floured surface and knead lightly about 3 or 4 times.
6. Roll dough to 1/2-inch thickness; cut into 36 rounds with a 2-inch cutter, and place on nonstick baking sheets.
7. Bake at 400° for 10 to 12 minutes.
   Yield: 36 biscuits Each serving: 1 biscuit

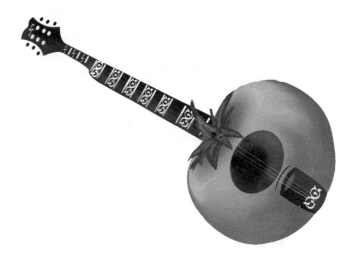

Roy's Apple Muffins

1-2/3 C all-purpose flour
2-1/2 tsp. baking powder
1/2 tsp. salt
Sugar substitute to equal
  1 Tbsp. sugar
1 tsp. cinnamon

1/4 tsp. nutmeg
1 egg, slightly beaten
2/3 C skim milk
1/4 C reduced-calorie
  margarine, melted
1 C apples, minced

Steps in preparation:
1. Sift flour, baking powder, salt, sugar substitute, and spices into
   medium mixing bowl.
2. Combine egg, milk, and margarine.
3. Add egg mixture to dry ingredients, blending only until flour is
   moistened.
4. Fold in apples.
5. Pour batter into 12 nonstick muffin cups, filling each two-
   thirds full.
6. Bake at 400° for 25 minutes.
   Yield: 12 muffins Each serving: 1 muffin

Shoji Tabuchi

A t a Roy Acuff concert in his native Japan, Shoji Tabuchi heard Howdy Forrester play *Listen to the Mocking Bird*. From that moment on, there was never a doubt as to his future. He arrived in San Fransisco in 1962 with $600, his fiddle and a burning desire to become a country music star.

From his first standing ovation on the stage of the Grand Ole Opry years ago, to his most recent standing ovation—which you can be sure occurred during his most recent show—Shoji and his fiddle have blown music lovers away.

You have to hear it to believe it, but it's the feeling of it that will finish you off and make you a Shoji Tabuchi fan forever. It's still wise to get a reservation if you want to see his show—there are not often empty seats in his 1,900-seat theatre on Shepherd of the Hills Expressway.

Even With "Fiddlin' Fame,"
Shoji Still Finds Food Fun!

TEMPURA BATTER FOR BASS FROM BULL SHOALS

1 cup flour
1/2 t. sugar
1/2 t. salt
white bass

1 egg
1 cup ice water
4 t. cooking oil

1. Beat all ingredients together to mix well.
2. Wipe white bass dry with paper towel. Dip in batter.
3. Fry in deep cooking oil at 380° to 390° until lightly brown.
Note: Ice water may be added or deleted to adjust thickness of batter.

DEEP FRIED BASS

yellow corn meal
seasoned salt or chili powder, to taste
ice water

1. Mix yellow corn meal with season salt or chili powder.
2. Cut bass into finger strips.
3. Place bass in a bowl of ice water and keep water very cold.
4. Roll bass in corn meal mixture.
5. Deep fry at 380° to 400° until brown. Enjoy!

When I was living in Bossier City, Louisiana, I learned how to make this fantastic dish I call Shoji's Louisiana Jambalaya. It can also be made with the wonderful sea food found in that part of the country.

Shoji's Louisiana Jambalaya

2 Tbsp. bacon fat
1 cup finely chopped onion
1 cup chopped green pepper
2 cloves garlic, minced fine
1 cup diced cooked chicken
1 cup diced ham
12 tiny pork sausages, cut in pieces
2-1/2 cups canned tomatoes, undrained

1 cup raw white rice
1-1/2 cups chicken broth
1/2 t. thyme
5 Tbsp. chopped parsley
1/4 t. chili powder
1-1/2 t. salt
1/4 t. freshly ground black pepper

Preheat oven to moderate (350° F)
Melt bacon fat in a large skillet and add the onion, green pepper and garlic. Cook slowly, stirring often, until the onion and pepper are tender. Add the chicken, ham and sausages and cook 5 minutes.
Add tomatoes with the liquid, rice, broth, thyme, parsley, chili, salt and pepper. Turn the mixture into a large casserole. Cover and bake until the rice is tender, about one and one-quarter hours.
Note: This dish may be baked for 1 hour, refrigerated and, at serving time, baked long enough to finish cooking the rice. Enjoy!

I love Teriyaki, and here's an old family favorite that we make on our outdoor grill.

Momma Tabuchi's Terrific Teriyaki

2 lbs. sirloin steak, about 1/4" thick (chicken breasts can be substituted)
1 Tbsp. finely chopped fresh ginger or 2 t. powered ginger
2 cloves garlic, chopped fine
1 medium onion (or scallion) chopped fine
2 Tbsp. sugar
1 cup soy sauce
1/2 cup sherry

Cut the steak into thin slices or strips.
Combine the ginger, garlic, onion, sugar, soy sauce and sherry and pour the mixture over the meat. Let stand one or two hours.
Thread the meat on skewers and broil quickly on both sides over charcoal. (You can also use a broiler). Serve with rice.

SONS OF THE PIONEERS

In 1932, when Roy Rogers co-founded the Pioneer Trio—which was soon renamed The Sons of the Pioneers—he didn't suspect he was giving creative birth to one of the oldest, on-going entertainment groups in the country. Members have changed, over the 60-plus, non-stop years the group has performed, but the current group boasts one member who has been with Sons of the Pioneers 42 years.

Now appearing at the Braschler Theatre, on Shepherd of the Hills Expressway, the group continues their tradition of great western music—with some big band sounds thrown in for fun. Their unique (and possibly never equaled) sound delivers a delightful flow of the best songs of the cowboys—from both the range and the silver screen.

Sons Of The Pioneers

Nevada "Hot-Ribs" Bar-B-Q Sauce

Dale and Margaret Warren

Ribs: Brown in hot oven 3 or 4 racks of ribs (cut in pieces), drain off fat and pour the Bar-B-Q sauce. Turn often, cook one hour.

Sauce: Heat in large Dutch oven.

1 C. wine vinegar	1 C. of cider vinegar
8 garlic cloves	4 tsp. dry mustard
8 bay leaves	4 tsp. salt
4 tsp. paprika	1/2 tsp cayenne pepper
6 C. tomato sauce	

Cook on medium heat for 30 minutes. Stir often.
Add:

4 Tbsp. of Worcestershire sauce	4 beef bouillon cubes
1/2 square (or cube) of butter	1/4 C. sugar
2 tsp. of liquid smoke	

Baked Country Ham With Mustard Sauce

Luther and Carolyn Nallie

10 - 12 lb. country-style or Virginia ham	1 bottle (1 pt, 12 oz.) ginger ale
2 Tbsp. chopped pecans	1/2 C. light brown sugar, firmly packed
2 Tbsp. sweet-pickle juice	Mustard Sauce (below)

1. First day: Place ham in large, deep roasting pan; cover completely with cold water. Let stand - at least 12 hours, or overnight. Next day: Wash ham in fresh water; dry with paper towels. Preheat oven to 350°F.

2. Place ham, fat side up, in roasting pan. Pour ginger ale over ham. Bake, covered, 3-1/2 to 4 hours, or until tender.

3. Remove from oven. With sharp knife, remove skin from ham; score fat, if desired.

4. Sprinkle ham with brown sugar and pecans, pressing lightly in fat. Drizzle with sweet-pickle juice.

5. Bake, uncovered, 30 minutes longer, until sugar melts and ham is glazed. Serve hot or cold, sliced thin on the diagonal. Serve with

mustard sauce. Makes 24 servings.

MUSTARD SAUCE

1/2 C. light brown sugar
   firmly packed
2 Tbsp. butter or
   margarine, softened

1/3 C. prepared mustard
2 eggs
1/3 C. cider vinegar

   1. In small, heavy saucepan, with rotary beater, beat sugar, mustard, eggs, and butter. Gradually beat in vinegar.

   2. Cook over low heat, stirring constantly, until slightly thickened - about 10 minutes.

   3. Serve cold, or at room temperature. Makes 1-1/2 cups.

"PRAIRIE TERIYAKI CHICKEN SALAD"

David Bradley

1 head Chinese "nappa" cabbage (chopped)
1 large bunch green onions (chopped)
1 can water chestnuts (chopped)
4 chicken breasts skinned and de-boned
1/4 cup soy sauce and 1/4 cup teriyaki
1/2 cup butter
2 pkg. Top Ramen noodles (smashed)
2 small pkg. of slivered almonds
2 Tbsp. sesame seeds

   Bake chicken breast in shallow pan, add soy sauce and teriyaki sauce. Bake on 350°F for about 45 minutes or until done. Cool chicken then cut up into cubes or strips. Melt butter, brown noodles, almonds, sesame seed. "Use only Top Ramen Noodles." after browning, add 1 seasoning packet from the Top Ramen. (You can use any flavor you prefer). Let this cool completely. In large bowl add the Chinese napa cabbage, chopped finely. Add chopped onions, water chestnuts, cooled chicken and noodle mixture. Mix with dressing.

Dressing for Salad: Add together

1/2 C. olive oil
   or vegetable oil
1/4 C. sugar

1/4 C. rice vinegar
2 Tbsp. soy sauce
Optional: 1 Tbsp. sesame oil

   Leave salad in covered bowl in refrigerator for 4 hours. Great main dish or salad.

SPLINTER MIDDLETON

A nine-year veteran of the 76 Music Hall's "Memory Makers" show, Splinter Middleton is no stranger to the heat—in the kitchen or in the footlights. He not only appears in the theatre's early afternoon show, "Down Home Country," but he is also a versatile singer who walked off with the top male vocal award in the first "New Star Challenge," which was emceed by Bob Eubanks in 1995 and taped for television.

Splinter claims he's married "to a real cook. And I have one little girl, who helps her mom bake cookies!"

Splinter Middleton's Old Settler's Beans

Brown 1/2 lb. hamburger
Cook 1/2 lb. bacon with
    1 medium onion

MIX ABOVE WITH:
2 cans pork 'n' beans
1 can red kidney beans
1 can white beans
1/3 cup brown sugar
1/3 cup white sugar
1-1/4 cup barbeque sauce
2 tbsp. molasses
1-1/4 cup ketchup
1/2 tbsp. chili powder
1 tbsp. dry mustard

Mix well and pour into large casserole dish. Bake at 350-degrees for one hour.

Green Bean Casserole

1 can green beans
1 can cream of mushroom soup
1/4 cup milk
1 can French fried onions

Mix first three together and add 1/2 can of fried onions. Pour into casserole dish and sprinkle remaining fried onions over top. Bake at 350-degrees for 30 minutes.

DEATH BY CHOCOLATE

1 pkg. brownie mix
1/4 cup Kahlua
2 boxes chocolate mouse
1 lg. tub Cool Whip
   (or 2 pints whipped cream)
5 Heath Bars, "crunched up"

In another bowl mix:
2 c. flour
3 tsp. baking soda
2 tsp. cinnamon
1 tsp. salt

   Mix and bake brownies according to directions on box. When
cooked, pour Kahlua over brownies and cool. Crumble a third of the
brownies into a large cake pan, then make layers with a third of
everything else...mousse, Cool Whip, and Heath Bars. Repeat two
more times and refrigerate for at least an hour.

TERRY SANDERS

You now know him as the "handyman"— and the very funny man, Homer Lee—of the Braschlers Music Show. But Terry Sanders has been tickling funny bones all over the Ozarks under a variety of aliases.

For three years in the early 80s he played a variety of characters at Silver Dollar City while earning a degree at SMS; he also portrayed "Zenus" and "Toby" in Shad Heller's Corn Crib Theatre; and he took over as "Melvin the Chicken Thief" on the Wilkinson Brothers show.

Since 1985, except for a series of famed "HeeHaw" shows, he has delighted audiences at the Braschler Music Show, which is now located on Shepherd of the Hills Expressway.

Terry Sanders – You Know Him Better As "Homer Lee"

DOUBLE LAYER PUMPKIN PIE

1 pkg. (3 oz.) Philadelphia Brand cream cheese (softened)
1-1/2 C. Cool Whip
2 pkg. (4 serving size) Jello vanilla flavor instant pudding pie filling

1 C. plus 1 Tbsp. cold Half and Half
1 Tbsp. sugar
1 graham cracker pie crust (6 oz.)
1 can (16 oz.) pumpkin
1 tsp. ground cinnamon
1/2 tsp. ground ginger
1/4 tsp. ground cloves

MIX: Cream cheese, 1 Tbsp. half and half and sugar with wire whisk until smooth. Stir in whipped topping. Spread on bottom of crust.

POUR: 1 cup Half and Half into mixing bowl. Add pudding mix. Beat with wire whisk until well blended, 1 to 2 minutes. Let stand 3 minutes.

STIR: in pumpkin and spices, mix well. Spread over cream cheese layer. Refrigerate at least 2 hours. Garnish with additional whipped cream.

DEDE'S EASY ROLLS

2 C. warm water
1 egg
1/2 C. sugar
6 C. flour

2 Tbsp. yeast
1 tsp. salt
1/4 C. oil

Mix well, let raise, re-mix. Roll into balls, dip into butter. Put into baking pan and bake at 400° for 20 minutes.

Broccoli Casserole

1 onion (chopped)
1 pkg. frozen chopped broccoli,
   thawed and drained

1 can mushroom soup
1 sm. jar Cheese Whiz
1-1/2 C. Minute Rice prepared per
   instructions

SAUTE: onions in butter, add soup, broccoli and Cheese Whiz.
Simmer 10 - 15 minutes. Mix rice and above in casserole pan, and
bake at 350° for 30 minutes.

Taco Soup

2 lb. hamburger
   (cooked and drained)
2 cans tomatoes
1 can beans (hot i.e. jalapeno)

1 onion (chopped)
1 pkg. taco mix
1 can hominy
1 can plain beans

   Mix in pot and bring to boil, and then simmer as you would with
any soup.

TOM BRUMLEY

One of the hottest steel-guitarists in the world calls Branson "home." Tom Brumley, son of Albert E. Brumley (songwriter: *I'll Fly Away*, *Turn Your Radio On* and others), is a legend in the music industry. His credits include: a seven-year stint as a Buck Owens' "Buckeroo," which produced 26 consecutive No.1 songs; 10 years with the late Ricky Nelson; and two years in the Desert Rose Band. During his career he has played "steel" on No. 1 songs for Merle Haggard, Reba McIntyre, Steve Wariner, Martina McBride, Janie Fricke and Dwight Yoakum—just to name a few!

The featured performer in the lively Brumley Music Show at the 76 Music Hall, Tom is joined by his two sons, Tommy and Todd, and a variety of talented musicians and vocalists who deliver one of the most satisfying musical experiences in town.

Snowball Salad

2 large tubs Cool Whip
1-1/3 c. sugar
5 mashed bananas
1 lg. can crushed pineapple, drained
1 8-oz. pkg. sour cream
1-1/2 c. chopped pecans
2 tsp. lemon juice
1 small jar maraschino cherries, drained and chopped

Mix together. Put in freezer and keep this frozen until ready to slice and eat.

Swiss-Style Vegetable Bake
(Makes 12 servings)

1 20-oz. pkg. frozen cauliflower, cooked and drained
1 10-oz. pkg. frozen chopped broccoli, cooked and drained
1 17-oz. can whole kernel corn, drained
1 17-oz. can cream style corn
1 can cream of celery soup
3 tbsp. butter or margarine, melted
2 cups shredded Swiss cheese
1-1/2 c. soft rye bread crumbs

In a large bowl, fold together cauliflower, broccoli, whole kernel corn, cream style corn, cheese and soup. Spoon into greased 3-qt. casserole dish.
In small bowl, toss together bread crumbs and melted butter. Sprinkle over vegetable mixture and bake at 375-degrees for 40 minutes, or until casserole is hot and bubbly.

Baked Chicken 'n' Butter and Cream
(makes 3 to 4 servings)

1/2 c. flour
1-1/2 tsp. salt
1/2 tsp. paprika
1/4 tsp. pepper

1 cut up frying chicken
1/4 c. butter
1/2 c. nonfat dry milk powder
1-1/2 c. hot water

Dip chicken into water. Coat with mixture of flour and seasonings. Put skin side up into 13x9x2-inch baking pan. Dot with butter. Bake at 425-degrees for 30 minutes (or until golden brown. Remove from oven and pour milk around chicken, and cover with aluminum foil.

Return to oven and bake at 350-degrees for 45 minutes.

Hummingbird Cake

3 c. flour
1 tsp. salt
1 tsp. cinnamon
1-1/2 c. vegetable oil
1 (8-oz.) can crushed
pineapple, undrained
1 c. chopped pecans or walnuts

2 c. sugar
1 tsp. soda
3 eggs, beaten
1-1/2 tsp. vanilla
2 chopped bananas
1/2 c. coconut (optional)

Combine dry ingredients in a large bowl. Add eggs and oil, stirring until dry ingredients are moistened. Do not use mixer! Stir in vanilla, pineapple, pecans and bananas. Spoon batter into three, well-greased and floured 9" layer cake pans. Bake at 350-degrees for 25 to 30 minutes. Cool completely.

Cream Cheese Frosting:
1 8-oz. pkg. cream cheese, softened
1/2 stick margarine, softened
1 c. chopped pecans
1 lb. box powdered sugar
3 tsp. sweet milk
1 tsp. vanilla

Cream together cream cheese and margarine. Add powdered sugar, milk and vanilla and beat until smooth. Add pecans. Spread frosting between cooled cake layers and on sides.

YAKOV SMIRNOFF

Yakov has a history of breaking new ground. He came to America when nobody could leave Russia—and started doing comedy when he barely spoke English! Then, Yakov left L.A. and immigrated to a new country—Branson, that it!.

With the move, Yakov began the change from the wide-eyed immigrant who didn't understand the difference between perfume and toilet water to the more sophisticated, wide-eyed husband and father who doesn't understand the difference between natural childbirth and torture. "I've been here for fifteen years and the reality is, the more I learn about American ways, the less I truly understand. In essence, I'm still doing what I always did...sharing my attempts at becoming a real American with the audience."

Some things never change. His father-in-law still calls Yakov's daughter "a little chip off the old Soviet Bloc," and Yakov still thinks Father's Day was invented by some relative of Karl Mark (Hallmark)... and he is still one of the funniest men in America today.

Summer Borscht a la Smirnoff (Serves 8 to 10)

This is a classic cold soup from Russia which can start off any meal or be served as a main course at lunch. It always tastes good served with a piroshki.

6 medium-size beets, peeled
10 cups cold water
juice of 3 medium-size lemons
3 tbsp. sugar
2 tsp. salt

3 eggs
1 cup milk
1 cup sour cream
1 cucumber, peeled, seeded and diced
1/4 cup minced fresh dill weed

Cut beets into halves. Place them in a large soup kettle with 10 cups of water and bring to a boil. Reduce heat and simmer partially covered until beets are tender, approximately 30 to 40 minutes. Skim foam from top and discard.

Remove beets from liquid with a slotted spoon, set aside and cool to room temperature. Grate the beets and return them to their cooking liquid, along with the lemon juice, sugar and salt. Return to the stove and simmer for 15 minutes. Remove from the heat and let soup cool for 15 minutes.

Beat eggs and milk together in a bowl. Gradually whisk 3 cups of the warm borscht into the eggs and milk. Pour this mixture slowly back into the remaining borscht. Cover the soup and refrigerate until very cold.

Taste and correct seasoning; the soup should be nicely balanced between sweet and sour. Ladle into chilled soup bowls. Garnish with sour cream, diced cucumber and fresh dill. Serve immediately.

Beef Stroganoff
(Serves 6)

This famous Russian dish, originally created for Count Stroganoff, tastes best served with buttered, wide noodles and a green salad.

2 lbs. sirloin tip or bottom round, trimmed of fat
3 tbsp. of butter
1 medium finely chopped onion
2 tbsp. of flour
2 beef bouillon cubes
1-3/4 cups of water
2 tbsp. of tomato paste

1 tsp. dry mustard or
  1 tablespoon Dijon-type mustard
1-1/2 tsp. of salt
Dash of freshly ground pepper
1/2 pound of mushrooms, thinly sliced
1/2 cup sour cream

Cut meat in strips about 1/2" thick and 1/2" wide. If round steak is used, marinate or simmer until tender. Cook meat quickly in butter, turning to brown evenly on all sides.

Remove meat, add onion and cook until onion is clear. Blend in flour, cooking until it browns lightly. Dissolve bouillon cubes in 1-3/4 cups water, then slowly stir into flour mixture. Continue to cook flour mixture until slightly thickened.

Add tomato paste, seasonings, mushrooms and meat. Cover and simmer about 30 minutes, or until meat is tender. Fold in sour cream and continue cooking only until mixture is heated through. Serve over cooked butter noodles.

CHICKEN YAKOV
(Serves 4)

I've changed this classic Russian entree by substituting yogurt for butter and leaving the bone in to form a natural pocket. It tastes just as good as my Mamulya used to make it, only lower in fat calories.

1/2 cup plain yogurt
1 clove garlic, minced
3 tbsp. snipped fresh chives
1/2 tsp. salt

Dash of freshly ground pepper
Pinch of cayenne pepper
4 skinless chicken breast halves,
  rinsed and patted dry.

Combine all ingredients except the chicken in a small bowl and mix well.

Holding a thin, sharp knife almost parallel to the bone, cut two diagonal slits in each breast, 2 inches apart, to form two pockets. Lift the flap of each pocket and fill it with some of the yogurt mixture.

Arrange the breast halves in a baking dish, and spoon any remaining filling on top. Cover loosely and refrigerate for one hour.
Preheat oven to 450. Bake the chicken until it is crisp and brown, about 35 minutes; serve right away.

Strawberries Natasha
(Serves 4 to 6)

Created in honor of my very sweet daughter, Natasha.

4 egg whites, at room temperature
1/4 tsp. salt
1/4 tsp. cream of tartar
1 cup fine granulated sugar
4 tsp. cornstarch
2 tsp. white wine vinegar
1 tsp. vanilla extract
1 cup heavy cream, chilled
2 to 3 cups strawberries, sliced and
    sprinkled with sugar
    (and Grand Mariner, if desired)

Preheat oven to 275. Beat egg whites, salt and cream of tartar together in a bowl until the whites hold a stiff peak. Add the sugar, a few tablespoons at a time, beating until mixture is stiff and glossy. Beat in the cornstarch, then the vinegar and vanilla. Butter and lightly flour a loose-bottomed 8-inch cake pan and fill gently with the meringue mixture, spreading it higher around the edges than in the center of the pan to form a depression. Bake it for 1 to 1-1/4 hours, or until meringue is firm and lightly browned. Cake will remain moist inside. Cool slightly, unmold, slide onto a serving plate and cool completely.

Lightly whip cream. Just before serving, spread the cake with whipped cream and then with strawberries. Serve immediately.

Branson's Cookin'!

With Branson's Celebrity Cookbook

Whether you call us the "Broadway of Country Music" or "The Music Show Capitol of the World," Branson Cooks with entertainment! And now you can catch your favorite star in the kitchen with"Branson's Celebrity Cookbook"…300 recipes and 200 pages of the stars who shine in Branson. There's no better way to get a taste of Branson than to order Branson's Star-Studded cookbook. And if you subscribe to **Branson's Review** Magazine, we'll pay for the shipping and handling of the cookbook (a 3^{00} value) So, clip the coupon below and mail payment to: **Branson's Review** Box 357, Branson, Mo 65615

Yes! I wish to order_____of Branson's Celebrity Cookbook(s) at $12.95 each (Shipping FREE!)

Name

Address

City

State   Zip

Circle if **MasterCard** or **VISA**   Card Number   EXP. DATE   / /

Signature

Yes, I also wish to subscribe to **Branson's Review** magazine and save $3 on my cookbook order.
Only $25.92 per cookbook magazine order.